CALLED TO THE "ONE"!

CALLED TO THE "ONE"!

The Ministry of Jesus

Brian Jacobson

XULON PRESS

Xulon Press
2301 Lucien Way #415
Maitland, FL 32751
407.339.4217
www.xulonpress.com

ISBN-13: 978-1-6312-9265-1

DEDICATION

To my bride and partner in spirit and life, Linda, who has inspired, encouraged, and challenged me to be the best I can be and to release these gifts of wisdom that God has shown me through lifes' lessons. She believed in me before I believed in myself. Thank you for your strength and courage to help me stay on this journey of faith and discovery with Jesus!

ACKNOWLEDGMENTS

A special thanks to Betsy & Chester Kylstra and the revelation of the Integrated approach. They welcomed me even before I had finished my healing, seeing my potential and helping me grow. Becoming part of Restoring the Foundations was like coming home and finding my tribe, who spoke the same language and carried a shared vision.

A special thanks to a prophetic friend of mine, Pat Ford, who spoke a word of truth and encouragement seven years ago that helped me gain confidence for this assignment.

And my greatest thanks to the Father, Jesus, and the precious Holy Spirit, who convey their heart to and through me every day! It's all about them, and seeing the Bride healed!

INTRODUCTION

Hello, friends of Restoring the Foundations (RTF) and Brian & Linda. For almost 14 years friends have encouraged me to write a book and to share what God has taught me over the years. It felt overwhelming to take on such a big task. My wife Linda had an idea that writing blogs (most recent ones posted on our website, HisHeartministers.com/blogs) might be a good way to start the process and help me begin to verbalize some of the nuggets of truth God has revealed to me over sixty years of living.

So here it is!

The subject matter includes items from seminars and teachings I have done over the past few years, Bible studies I am working on, or some of the revelations He has given me in the ministry room. A major focus has been the condition of the Heart and applying the RTF principles to the heart needs. We have seen significant results with marriages, having had eighty-plus couples who have been separated up to two years, and all of them are back together but three. We have taught about God's design for marriage, sexual purity, intimacy vs. surviving, the "normalcy" of doing spiritual warfare, Biblical equality in marriage, and so much more.

As I sit down to write, I trust God will light a spark of new revelation and understanding of His truth that leads to increased freedom. He called Linda and I to "*the one*", which is the Ministry of Jesus (that's a story all in itself!), and I hope writing this collection of articles will help release the incredible wisdom and revelations He has blessed me with over the years. Of course, *you* are responsible to run it through your own spirit and the Holy Spirit as to how you hear it and respond to it.

The Lord said, "*He who is faithful in the little, I will give him even more.*" (Luke 16:10; Matt 25:23) This is a prophetic journey of trust and learning to hear the Lord even better. Here is an excerpt from Revelation #9, in Chapter 3: "*God doesn't trust me because I am trustworthy. I become trustworthy because He trusts me. His trust changes me! The love and trust we extend to one another changes both the one who trusts and the one who is trusted in the process. When we are trusted it helps us know we are loved, special, valued, and honored. It feeds us and helps us grow.*" This is just one example of hundreds that the Lord has taught me that are life changing.

I look forward to sharing this journey with you and welcome whatever the Lord shows you. This compilation is the first of three volumes that I believe God wants me to release. Much love and blessing to all!

Brian Jacobson,
RTF minister and trainer.

TABLE OF CONTENTS

CHAPTER 1

BEGINNINGS

Revelation #1: *The Un-veiling of the Ministry of "The One"*

"For God so loved the world..." —John 3:16

Fifteen years ago, while we were watching some friends of ours being prayed over by some prophets, the Lord spoke to me some words that would come to change my life and my thinking. As the prophet was saying to our friends, "God has called you to the ninety-nine. You are going to touch the multitudes," and so forth, I heard the Holy Spirit speak to my spirit, *"But I've called you to the one!"* When I heard that, my thoughts were, "Great, I'm not good enough for the ninety-nine. I'm just left with the dregs. God isn't going to use me for anything important at all." I had been removed as a pastor just two years before this and had felt like I was "thrown away," so I already had a rather negative disposition about my calling.

After the service, Linda asked me, "Did God say anything to you?" and I said, "Yes, He said we are called to the One." I wasn't exactly thrilled by it. Then she said, "That's exactly what I heard!" and she was very excited that we heard the same thing from the Lord. It wasn't until two years later, when we were getting ready to come to North Carolina for RTF training, when I was telling my pastor about this word about being "called to the one," he said to me, "Didn't you know? The Ministry of the One *is* the Ministry of Jesus!" Something changed in that moment.

Over the next few years, God began to show me more and more about what that really means. As we've ministered with Restoring the Foundations for the last fourteen years, He has shown me that He wants me to do ministry the way He does, up close and personal; to be willing to walk in another's shoes, without judgment, to speak truth in love; to accept them right where they are yet love them too much to leave them there. Jesus always meets us where *we* are, not the other way around.

It reminded me of where Jesus went immediately after dying on the cross. He went to *hell*! He went to where the broken and the lost were, to bring the good news of forgiveness and love to them *right where they were*! He didn't ask them to get cleaned up before they could come to Him, like many of us have believed. When Jesus died, Scripture says the curtain in front of the Holy of Holies in the temple was rent from top to bottom (Matt 27:51). Some historians believe the curtain was thirty-foot-wide and six inches thick, and it was totally torn apart; and because of it we now had *full* access to the very throne of God's grace, the Mercy Seat. Unfortunately, according to some historians, the Jewish leadership sewed the curtain back up. Once again, religious leaders put up walls between man and God, just like the Catholic confessional and other religious beliefs that say you can't go directly to God. Praise God that He didn't *"send His son into the world to condemn the world, but that it might be saved through Him!"* (Jn 3:17).

As I train other ministers, I tell them this is an important character for an RTF minister, that Jesus is inviting them to do ministry the way He does it. Most people have heard lots of sermons *telling* them what to do, what to believe, that they must repent to man and clean up their lives before God will have anything to do with them. But how many of those ministers were willing to come alongside them and walk with them on their journey of healing and transformation? This is a high calling!

Jesus modeled for me how valuable and honorable is the "Ministry of *the One*," and I'm grateful that He has called me to such a worthwhile ministry. Thank you, Lord!

Revelation #2: *"His Heartministers" Origins*

"For I have to be about my Father's business..." –Luke 2:49

"His Heartministers" is the name God gave us for our ministry about sixteen years ago. We had recently left working with Good Samaritan Ministries, an international counseling agency in Portland, Oregon. I had gone there after being thrown away as a pastor in Seattle, after my wife had left, and after I felt I'd lost everything in my life. God began my journey of healing there, and eventually I became the director of their half-way house, where I had come to live.

Two years later, I was exposed to Theophostic Ministry and experienced a touch to my heart like nothing I'd ever known, encountering Jesus deeper than any time in my thirty-five years as a Christian. It was the beginning of a deeper search for a truly personal relationship with Him, to experience His powerful life-changing presence. Friends we met there told us about House of Myrrh Ministries and their Heart Change workshop and that it would be very beneficial for us. It is a four-day intensive work-shop of experiencing the Father-heart of God. It led to us going on staff with them and presenting workshops for the next three years. I became their counseling supervisor and was creating a training program for other ministers.

It was in that time frame that we came up with the name: _His Heartministers._ Everything is about our hearts and His! He wanted us to minister with His heart for others! Jesus often referred to doing ONLY what the Father led him to do. _"I have to be about my Father's business."_ (Luke 2:49) We wanted to follow the same leading.

When He led us to Restoring the Foundations, where we have been ministering full time for the past fourteen years, this name would prove to be a true representation of who _we_ are, and the anointing and calling He had prepared us for! Since then, He has been teaching us to do ministry the way He does it, _up close and personal_. He has enabled and empowered us to come alongside others in their brokenness, and to link arms with them as He lovingly invites them to come out of the darkness and into His great light.

Eight years ago, while teaching at a church in New York, their prophetic team prayed over us and said God was delighted in our ministry because we _"revered"_ the hearts of men. He went on to say we had a kind of "grandparent" anointing. God was con-firming to us that He cares about the hearts of His children more than anything and that we were honoring Him as we honored His children with sensitive and caring hearts.

"His Heartministers" has come to be a true representation of who Linda and I are and, I hope, a reflection of who He is. We are honored to be chosen as His Heart Ministers. We are grateful for the hundreds of lives we've had the privilege to walk alongside, some for a season and some for a lifetime! In the process, we have met many of our gracious, loving family members from all over the world. As my pastor from Seattle often said, "We are melding our heart-strings together," and it is a beautiful thing.

Revelation #3: *"One Plus One Does Not Equal Two!"*

"For my thoughts are not your thoughts, neither are your ways my ways," declares the Lord. "As the heavens are higher than the earth, so are my ways higher than your ways and my thoughts than your thoughts." —Isaiah 55:8–9

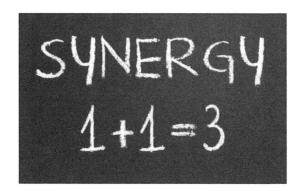

I had some new revelation last night that I'm still unraveling. I felt like the Lord was having me think about some friends' marriage material (Dave & Linda Roeder's The Intimate Marriage), and how when one person is connected or joined to another person, together they become something altogether different. I kept seeing one person's name merged with another, and instead of becoming the same name it became something else altogether, like a sound or an aroma. What were two pieces of matter transformed into another component altogether when it came together. It changed its physical makeup and became a sound, a smell, a wave, something beyond just what our normal senses could take in or fully comprehend.

This dream reminded me of C.S. Lewis' book *The Great Divorce*, which tells a story of a man who dies and goes to this place where everything is *so* real, *so* solid that he is almost like a ghost. As this man spent more time there, he became more and more solid and able to interact with the new world he was in. I believe Lewis was trying to help us grasp the truth that God's kingdom and reality is so much more *real* than our reality or our ability to perceive reality! That may be part of what God was trying to show me in this revelation, where His Kingdom is intersecting our present reality and changing it; or at the least, helping us be able to perceive more of what is already His reality here on earth.

When I was sharing this with Linda and trying to unravel what this meant, I felt it was a new revelation about marriage, about the church, about worship, about the *transformation* process of us being supernaturally changed into something different that would allow us to truly communicate and commune with God's Spirit. It was then that it struck me that one plus one does *not* equal two! One piece of human matter connected to another piece of human matter doesn't just become a bigger piece of matter but of something else altogether, such as sound and light and smell. It dawned on me that when we come together as the church or the body of Christ, our very gathering changes us; and there is a new *sound* created just by our presence with each other in the Spirit.

It's not about the sound we are making with our voices or that we hear with our ears but a sound we make with our spirits when we resonate with His Spirit; and the waves go out around the universe. Just like certain sounds that dogs hear but we can't, this sound wave can only be heard by the ears of our spirits as He plays the strings of our hearts like an instrument. When we come together in unity and one accord there is a sound and an aroma that resounds in the spiritual world and can only be registered with spiritual ears. We are the instrument and He is the musician.

Even secular science knows about the reality of many ranges of both light waves and sound waves that are beyond our ability to register with our human eyes and ears. But what was exciting to me was that our very being and spirit were releasing these sounds into the universe by being in each other's presence and Him changing our very essence. I know it sounds mystical and mysterious and almost unreal, but it totally makes sense! One plus one does *not* equal two but something beyond math or mass or matter altogether. It is like an explosion of light and sound that is aligned with God's creation and there is a celebration of one-ness and joy that can't be measured! And as we are changed, we are *never* the same again! We are being changed from "*corruptible to Incorruptible, from mortal to immortal*" (I Cor. 15:51–54).

Perhaps this is what our souls cry out for, to be like Him, to be with Him, to enjoy fellowship with Him! I feel like He wants us to experience more of this in our marriages, our families, our church fellowships, and throughout the entire body of Christ that is *one* big network of heartstrings with Him! Can you imagine a harp with two million strings, all resonating in tune with the other as the Master Musician plays it? What a sound! What a powerful resonating, pulsating, penetrating wave of love and light that would wash over this creation! Is that not what the earth cries out for? Wow!

For this to work, it seems we would need to be close in proximity to each other and to be perfectly tuned and aligned with each other. I don't imagine there can be much harmony and unity if we are all orphans, full of walls and judgments, fearful and mistrusting of one another, jealous and competitive and bitter with each other. If we are to be this *instrument* of change throughout the world, we need the healing and freedom to come together as *one* voice, *one* sound, *one* symphony, led by *one* Director, Jesus Christ. What a glorious composition it will be.

I know this is a new revelation for me, if not for anyone else, and I am excited to explore this new realm, to open myself up to Him, the creator of all life, to become the *"new creation"* He describes in 2 Cor. 5:17. There have been so many words lately from Chuck Pierce and others who used the words, "a *new* thing," and if it is truly *new*, then we have never seen it before and may not even recognize it! Lord, give us hearts and spirits to supernaturally recognize this *new* thing you are doing, and to join in the celebration of your *"glorious inheritance in the saints!"* (Eph. 1:14).

Revelation #4: *"The Day God Blew Up My Cave"*

"You are my hiding place; you preserve me from trouble. You surround me with songs of deliverance." –Psalm 32:7

Have you noticed how popular the idea of the "man cave" is? Where a man can go to hide and watch sports to his heart's content? Where he can avoid his wife or family or burdens or worries? This whole notion is about how to cope with the stress and burdens of this world, to find a way to lessen it or to numb out from it. It also serves the need to find a *safe* place in which we can release our burdens.

For most of us, we have a place we go to in our minds when we feel stressed or anxious, a place where we can go to regroup or reenergize or just to rest from the burdens we are surrounded by. For some, this escape is into busyness or games or sports or activities or addictive behaviors like shopping or drinking or sex or porn. When things get tough, we literally check out and dissociate from life, both physically and emotionally.

My personal way of dealing with the pain and hardness of life was to go to what I called my "cave". For my wife, she called it "going to my room," because that was what was familiar to her growing up. Having been on this journey of healing for over forty years, God has been inviting me to stay present and to not escape when things get hard, to choose to trust Him instead. One day as I was talking with Him about this and revisiting my familiar place, my cave, He chose to blow up my cave! Now what do I do? How do I cope or survive while surrounded by pain and confusion? He simply invited me to trust Him, come to Him, welcome Him into the situation, and to release all the fear and pain to Him! Are you kidding? Who do you think I am some kind of saint or something? It was terrifying at first, but because Jesus and I had built a lifetime of trust I could learn from Him the truth that it was important for me to get rid of my escape mechanism and choose to stay present, in the present!

Like the story of Cortez and how he burnt his ships so that his soldiers would be forced to have to fight for their lives because there was no retreat, I too was forced to deal with the present issues head-on. It was this level of desperation that permitted Cortez and his army the ability to conquer the Mayan dynasty that had held on to its kingdom for over four hundred years. Jesus wanted me to know the same level of desperation and ability to conquer things in my own life and to have the power and motivation to follow it through, even to death!

This level of training for life and warfare may seem dramatic and extreme, but not only are we in a battle, we also need to know that we have the victory, *if* we will leave our caves and march into our true destiny and glorious future with Him! He is inviting us from survival into true living, which involves risk but also involves great joy and excitement on the adventure. I hope you will make a new choice to allow Him to come in and to step out of whatever comfort place you may escape to, knowing that life with Him is far richer and exciting. The present *is* the present, and it's time to embrace it and celebrate the gift that it is!

CHAPTER 2

LOVE!

Revelation #5: *You cannot escape His Grace*

"For it is by grace you have been saved through faith—and this is not from yourselves, it is a gift from God." —Ephesians 2:8

G race is a term that is controversial to many. Recently, someone talked about a church that was too grace centered. Apparently, they were thinking that they were operating in what we used to call "greasy grace," a term that implies turning a blind eye to anything, just accepting a person's behaviors and choices without any consequence. On the other side of the spectrum are the more legalistic churches that focus on hell and damnation, that we are all garbage and deserve punishment.

Pastor Bill Johnson of Bethel Church in Redding, California, shared a word that may shed some light on these diverse viewpoints. He said it is the difference between the Old testament perspective and the New Testament perspective. In the OT view, the focus is on our sinfulness and how the sinful nature defiles us and those around us, just like touching the leper for instance. In the NT view, we are no longer defiled by another's sin. Instead of being defiled by touching the leper, we can now touch the leper and see him healed! *"Sin is defeated in sinful man..."(Romans 8:3)* God is certainly *NOT* intimidated by our sin!

This hit home for me when I was reading about the *"accuser of the brethren"* in Revelation 12:10 and how he *"accused men before God, day and night."* What dawned on me was the thought, "If Satan, who is so evil and rebellious against God, can be in His presence, then why is it that I am too dirty to be in His presence?" It seemed so clear how ridiculous it was for me to believe that I could not come before my Heavenly Father!

A couple of years ago, God taught us a lesson about grace during a ministry session (and we have the permission of this person to share it with you). We were going through some forgiveness issues, and she was having a hard time forgiving herself. Sound familiar? God took her to a waterfall and told her to go under it. As she did, she saw black stuff washing off her into the river. Even though she saw this cleansing going on, she said, "It's just not enough! I'm still too dirty. This isn't going to work!" And I'll never forget God's response to her! He showed her a picture of just how vast the waterfall was, and as He panned the picture out, she could see the waterfall went on for miles, beyond what the eye could see. He said to her these priceless words, *"You cannot escape my grace!"*

We have often heard words like, "You cannot escape your sinfulness. It will always catch up with you until you pay for it in full." We have often been taught that we must clean ourselves up before we can go to Him. God was *not* minimizing the sin. The consequences of sin are still death! BUT, He was making it clear that our sin compared with His grace is like a drop of water in the ocean. His grace is so vast, our sin doesn't stand a chance against it. It speaks to the bigness of His love and how big is the gift He is offering us of salvation and forgiveness through the sacrificial blood of Jesus on the Cross! *"You cannot escape my grace!"* Words I will never forget!

Perhaps it would be helpful for us to step back a little and ask God for the bigger picture, to stop judging, and to allow Him to show us a truer perspective about people's hearts. We still need to repent of our sin and to receive His forgiveness, but as Isaiah 43:25 reminds us, *"I have forgiven your sins for My own sake, and will not remember them anymore!"* echoing the words of the Psalmist, *"As far as the East is from the West, so far have I removed your sins,"* and Paul to the Romans, chapter 1, *"There is Now no condemnation for those who are in Christ Jesus."* Do you think God is trying to make a point here? It is only from the perspective of this truth that we can be free to walk out our destiny as His beloved kids! Thank you, Lord. If you want to read a story or see a play that portrays this truth about His incredible grace, read or watch _Ragman_, by Walter Wangerin.

Revelation #6: Discovering the meaning of 'Restored Innocence' while climbing Mt. Sinai.

> *"For all have sinned and fallen short of the glory of God, and ALL are justified freely by His grace through the redemption that came by Christ Jesus..." —Romans 3:23-24*

This scripture can be a great equalizer, helping us know that we all stand before God with the same brokenness and that none of us has a right to think we are better than another. However, there is more to the story.

During one of the darkest times of my life, almost twenty-five years ago, I learned a truth that would change and shape my identity and my destiny. I was pastoring a Free Methodist Church in Washington State and loving it. I had been married about six-teen years and thought my wife was on board with my calling and assignment, but she wasn't! We had struggled off and on with understanding each other for most of our marriage, having gone to dozens of counseling sessions. What we didn't know at the time was that our communication styles were so different we kept wounding each other with our words and responses. I was primarily an external processor and she was dominantly an internal processor (that's a whole other teaching I write about in chapter 7). It created a lot of misunderstanding and pain, which ultimately, we were unable to overcome.

After sixteen years, she decided she'd had enough and wanted a divorce. When I came back from a weekend retreat, I found she had just moved out with all her stuff. I didn't even know she was going to do it. I was crushed and broken and felt a pain I didn't know you could feel. Eventually, it led to another crushing blow, the church dismissing me as a pastor. I felt like I'd literally lost everything. This momentous event felt like the end of the world, but it actually was the beginning of some true healing and release from a life of brokenness, fear, and shame.

An elderly friend of mine, Joe Cooke, who had been a sup-porter for me during seminary, invited me to come to Portland and meet with a counselor who could minister to my broken heart. That started me on a journey of healing that would cul-minate two years later with me climbing Mt. Sinai in Egypt. I had been going to group sessions and individual sessions of therapy around these hurts, learning to take responsibility for my part in the failure of the relationship. I wrote a series of letters to my ex-wife and her responses to them. After the fifth letter, the Lord said to send it. Her response to the letter was exactly what I had already written as led by the Holy Spirit, and I knew that I had finished this key step of owning up to my part, understanding what I had done, and asking forgiveness for it.

Six months after that letter, I went on a trip to Israel and Egypt. As I was climbing Mt. Sinai, the Holy Spirit spoke to my heart in a perfectly clear voice, *"I declare you innocent!"* From that moment on, I've never carried an ounce of guilt, regret, shame, or fear around the divorce and all the heartbreak that followed. I was totally *free* to move forward with my life, my calling, and my destiny. God took my shame and guilt in such a powerful and personal way. I experienced His power and love in a way I had never known.

Many of us stay stuck in Romans 3:23 and miss the next statement in 3:24, which says, *"Are justified freely by His grace through the redemption that came by Jesus Christ."* In other words, He declares us innocent when washed in His blood. As Paul says later in Ephesians 2, *"For it is by grace you have been saved, through faith—and this not from yourselves, it is the gift of God—not by works, so that no one can boast."* God delights in setting us free from the burden of guilt and shame! He does not delight in punishing us or beating us up but only wants the very best for us as His children.

The truth of His grace met me at my most broken place as I got honest with Him. And the truth of His word in Isaiah 43:25 resonated loudly: *"I, even I, am He who blots out your transgressions, for My own sake, and remembers your sin no more!"* As we say to others when they finish affirming their Godly Identity statements, "If God said it, that settles it!" Thank you, Lord.

Revelation #7: *Psalm 103*

Today, God woke me up from a dream and kept hammering in my mind, *"Psalm 103!"* I felt He was showing me someone's life (who I couldn't make out) and that even though they didn't know what this Psalm said, it was the words that defined their life. They had many hurts and losses, but these words were the truth about who they were and what God said about them. In the dream it was like God was trying to get this person to look at this unknown scripture in order to reveal to them what had always been their reality, but they never knew it; almost like it had been hidden to them and was now being revealed. It was *always* the truth, it was always *the* truth, but this person could only see the hard and bad stuff instead. I felt a great pressure in my chest and felt like my heart was going to beat out of my chest. I *had* to get up and look at what Psalm 103 said, as if my life depended on it!

> *"Praise the Lord, o my soul; all my inmost being, praise His holy name. Praise the Lord, o my soul; and forget not all His benefits: who forgives all your sins and heals all your diseases, who redeems your life from the pit and crowns you with love and compassion, who satisfies your desires with good things so that your youth is renewed like the eagle's." (Ps 103:1-5)*

This psalm is an awesome Word, but often feels like a pipe dream. Is this really the truth? Is this how God sees my life and reality? Can I trust these statements and promises? Or are they for someone other than me? How do I take hold of such statements of faith and promise? Are these just some future heavenly reality that I will never know on this earth?

v. 3–"He heals all my diseases?" (When? How? What about my diabetes, or Linda's stroke?)

v. 3–"He forgives all my sins?" (What about my bad habits or impatience or chronic sin?)

v. 4–"He crowns me with love and compassion?" (Is that really my reward, my identity?)

v. 4–"He redeems my life from the pit?" (How come I'm still depressed, lonely, fearful, and burdened?)

v. 5–"He satisfies my desire with good things?" (Instead of lust, perversion or selfish desires?)

v. 6–"The Lord works righteousness and justice for all the oppressed." (What about all those being persecuted, tortured, abused, and victimized around the world? How is justice being worked out? When will they see justice?)

v. 8 &10 – "The Lord is compassionate and gracious, slow to anger, abounding in love…"; "He does not treat us as our sins deserve or repay us according to our iniquities."

v. 11–"For as high as the Heavens are above the earth, so great is His love for those who fear Him."

v. 12 – *"As far as the east is from the west, so far has He removed our transgressions from us."* "But GOD…" appears 3,940 times in His word. What's your "but"? Do you play the 'what-if' game?

None of this will make any sense unless you encounter this living God. Your head can't translate this truth. Only your heart and soul, connected to Jesus, can know this reality and find encouragement and strength from its truth!

Our inmost beings are crying out to praise Him. It is what we were built for. They are screaming to be let out and acknowledge the mysteries of God's greatness and goodness and glory. We serve a big, huge, amazing, incredible, extravagant, incredulous, outrageous, fantabulous God. Why do we think of Him with such small thinking? God wants us to believe for and live based on this truth that far exceeds our puny view of Him and of life. He invites us to come higher, to risk greater, to believe for the impossible, to trust Him for the miraculous, and for the supernatural to become the natural. How outrageous is that!

I must admit, much of my life has been filled more with fear and rejection rather than faith and hope. But I can't deny the reality of encountering the living God, and what I have experienced of Him is so much bigger than I could ever describe with words! Perhaps that is why Ps 103 is so important. He describes the extravagance of His love for us, and then later He demonstrates it through His great sacrifice of His son, Jesus, on the cross. Here is another story, another passage that speaks to the power of the Cross and the shed blood of Jesus, and the incredible outcome that was accomplished for our eternal life through it. We sang last Sunday the song "His love is extravagant," and perhaps that is the lens we need to read this psalm through.

When He woke me up, there was an urgency in taking hold of this revelation of His goodness and love that I needed to grasp somehow. It is my prayer that as we continue to press into Him, we might grasp *"how wide and high and long and deep is the love of Christ"* (Eph 3:18). His sacrifice is the gateway to encountering Papa God's love as we now have *"full access to the throne of grace"* (Heb 4:14–16). Welcome to His reality and His kingdom.

Revelation #8: *"I Love You!"—Recognizing the REAL thing.*

"LOVE is…" —I Corinthians 13

Happy Valentines' Day to all who love!

Why do we need an official holiday to tell us when to express love to our spouse, family, or friends? Does this holiday say, "I love you"? Does "I love you" even mean anything anymore?

Love; is this an overused term today? Agape, phileo, eros—what's it gonna be? Ooey-gooey love? Tough love? Syrupy love? Puppy love? Friendship love? True love? Undying love? A mothers' love?

When someone says, "I love you," can you trust it? Or is it just a cliché, something someone says out of obligation? When someone says, "I love you," we often think, "Yeah, right! What do You really want? What are the strings attached to these words?" What are the strings attached to these words? What do they expect from me? Is there such a thing as pure love, a love with no strings attached? How can we ever be sure if someone really means it when they say these words? Can we risk opening our hearts and being vulnerable?

God has a lot to say about love, and it seems extravagant and incredible, almost too good to be true. *"Love is patient, love is kind…love never fails"*; *"My love for you knows no limit"*; *"For God SO loved the world that He gave His only begotten son"*; *"Love the Lord your God with all your heart, soul, mind, and strength; and love your neighbor as yourself"*; *"That you might know how wide, how long, how high, how deep is the love of God"*; *"Jesus love me, this I know, for the Bible tells me so"*; *"Above all other virtues, put on love, which binds them all together"*; *"God is love; whoever lives in love, lives in God, and He in them"*; *"Love covers a multitude of sins"*; *"There is no greater love than this, that a man would lay down his life for another."*

There are many ways the Bible talks about love without even using the word, such as, *"My thoughts about you are more than sands of the seashore"* (Ps 139), and *"For the joy set before Him, Christ endured the cross"* (Heb 12).

Love is action. Love is sacrifice. Love is a choice. Love is a gift. Love is costly. Love is confusing. Love can hurt. Love is emotion. Love is an attitude. Love is a person.

Love is invisible like the wind, but its power is mightier than any other force. One can have the *"faith to move mountains, but without love it is nothing."* (I Cor 13:2)

If God is love, then why does He allow so much suffering? This question has been asked by almost every living soul. Why such pain? Is that the message of His love? Many of us have heard the line, "It is better to have loved and lost than to have never loved at all." When our hearts are broken from a betrayed love, how do we cope with it? When someone we love dies, what happens to the love that was there? It seems so confusing and impossible. What about the Cross of Christ? Is it a symbol of love? Or is it just a symbol of pain and loss?

Our hearts long for love the way our lungs long for every single breath. Without it, our lives mean nothing. Without it, no amount of success or money or anything has any value. Without love, death itself seems attractive! Where can we find this love? How do we access this powerful spirit? How do we even know if it is real? Or whether it can be trusted? How many books have been written about love or with love as a key ingredient? Would we have any of the millions of romantic novels that have been written? And are not tragedies filled with love or the loss of love? Is not love the core of any story line?

When I say, "I love you" to my wife, what am I trying to convey? When I say these words to my brother at church, what do I want him to know? What is the heart message I want them to receive? Is it, "You are important to me, you are special, I care about you, I value you, you mean more to me than anything, I need you, I adore you," and so forth? Or, is it just because you like something they did? How often do we hear these words on shows like *The Voice*, when the coaches say, "I love you"? What they are really saying is, "I love your talent and I want it for myself."

Pure love, extravagant love, tender love, sacrificial love, love that lasts, are they a myth? Are they worth seeking out? Are they worth investing in? Are they worth giving everything for? I hope so! I hope the love I give and the love I receive will be all of these. If I am tapped into the true Vine, will this not be the fruit of my connection with the source of all love? "*I love because He first loved us*" (I Jn 4:19).

My heart feels and embraces this love; and my prayer would be that my life would be remembered for how I loved deeply.

I love you and I mean it! I hope your heart receives the message and takes it in. (See Graham Cooke's YouTube, "Love Encounter": https://youtu.be/Y6wlClByBG8)

CHAPTER 3

HEALING

Revelation #9: *Mistrust: an Un-recognized Form of Abuse*

"Trust in the Lord with all your heart…" – Proverbs 3:5

In a previous revelation, I talked about going through a divorce and how God brought me to a place of healing and an understanding of restored innocence. During that process of healing I had to answer the question "How have I contributed to the breakdown and failure of this relationship?" As I spent many weeks and months of processing the pain and the shame, writing some letters about what my part was, the Lord said to me, *"You didn't trust. Mistrust equals* abuse*!"* I had never heard anything like that before. God began to show me what it was like to be on the other end of a relationship where one doesn't trust the other and how it makes them feel. Mistrust is very destructive and hurtful to the partner and causes friction and fractures in the oneness that marriage is designed to be (and *any* intimate relationship or friendship).

God has been working on my trust issues most of my life, over fifty years now as a believer. As the child of an alcoholic father (an ACOA), I grew up not trusting because of the abandonment I experienced from my dad. The insecurity that developed from the lack of a role model, the lack of nurture, and the lack of security and guidance just reinforced that mistrust. I believe the core lesson God has been trying to teach me is that *all* trust comes from my relationship with Him and whether I trust Him! We are not trustworthy by nature, but we *become* trustworthy because He trusts us. His trust changes us.

Trust is a powerful change agent for Building us up. In my case, my mistrust had the effect of tearing down the intimacy, security, and oneness that God desired for my marriage. In some sense, my mistrust became a form of self-sabotage, and I didn't have a clue it was going on. It was like an invisible disease, eating away at the most sensitive and precious parts of my heart. Believing lies about my partner and listening to the mocker's voice helped feed that spirit of mistrust. What I've learned through RTF is that when we come against the mocker with spiritual warfare, change what we believe about our spouse, and affirm God's identity over one another, we can build intimacy rather than tear it down.

Growing up in a world filled with sarcasm and mockery, my sensitive heart didn't thrive very well. Thankfully, God has been teaching me very practically how to keep my sensitivity, while strategically coming against the true enemy of my heart. Paul said in Ephesians 6:12, *"Your enemy is NOT against flesh and blood, but against the powers and principalities of this dark world,"* and in 2 Corinthians 10:3–5, *"For though we live in the world, we do not wage war as the world does. The weapons we fight with are not the weapons of the world. On the contrary, they have divine power to demolish strongholds! We demolish arguments and every pretension that sets itself up against the knowledge of God, and we take captive every thought to make it obedient to Christ."* God has been revealing what true meekness can be, sensitive and graceful, but powerful and courageous! This is the modeling Jesus demonstrated for us and that we are now invited to live by.

Mistrust is the enemy of our hearts. It comes from old hurts, iniquity, traumatic experiences, stinking thinking, and demonic assault. As God heals us and changes our heart and we learn how to have appropriate boundaries, this old enemy will no longer be able to steal our most treasured gifts, each other's hearts.

Revelation #10: "*The Jail Cell of Un-forgiveness*"

"Forgive us our debts as we forgive our debtors..."
—Matthew 6:9

"Forgive one another as Christ has forgiven you..."
—Ephesians 4:32

Last fall I went for some personal ministry to deal with some of the trauma and hurt I still carried from the previous year of dealing with Linda's stroke and the hospital's negligence and all the stress that came with that journey. Having been sick myself and almost dying seven years before of pancreatitis, I knew what it was like to face death and be the sick one. However, being the caregiver of someone who was deathly ill was a whole other ballgame. There was so much hurt, anger, fear, and trauma associated with it all that I had to go on blood pressure and anxiety medicine. I even ended up in the hospital myself with a panic attack experience of my own. I needed help!

As I was receiving ministry, I was invited to do some forgiving by seeing the person I was forgiving in a jail cell, taking the key, and unlocking the door. In one instance, I was forgiving my father for the abandonment and neglect I had experienced by him as an alcoholic father. I envisioned him in a cell and was taking the key to open the cell when I saw Jesus in the cell with my father. As I shared this with my counselor, he quoted the scripture, *"In as much as you have done to the least of these, you have done unto me."* Wow! I had no idea I was putting Jesus in jail when I didn't forgive my father; that Jesus identified my dad as *"the least of these."* I didn't want to put Jesus in jail. It blew me away that Jesus would stand with my dad even when he was such a miserable wretch. It humbled me and impressed on me how much He really does love *all* of us, no matter how low we may have fallen or feel about ourselves.

While doing the same exercise around forgiving myself, I experienced the same thing as with my dad; Jesus was there with me in my jail cell. Though I knew I could open the jail cell, it was hard to let myself out and to believe I deserved to be released from my imprisonment. It was easier to hold on to the distorted perspective that I was safer or more comfortable in this prison of my own making, rather than risking getting hurt outside of it. It reminded me of a word spoken to me at a Heart-Change workshop sixteen years ago, where someone experienced me as someone in a jail cell with the door wide open, but I wouldn't come out. The difference this time, in seeing Jesus in jail with me, was the reality that it was my own will that kept Jesus locked up with me. That made it easier to make a new choice, to risk stepping outside the cell and embracing life, with all its risks and fears and unknown possibilities and dangers.

There was a time on my journey with Jesus that He blew up the "cave" I used to escape to. This was a similar experience, with Him inviting me to choose life and to step into a greater level of trusting Him. While it is mildly terrifying at times, I am choosing to press forward to a new level of trust as I walk in my gifting and anointing. He is turning up the heat and strongly impressing on me to take this leap of faith and see what He has for Linda and me, personally and in ministry.

Revelation #11: *Divine Healing is a process–never late and always complete!*

"For I am the Lord who heals you." –Exodus 15:26

"The Lord is not slow in keeping His promise, as some understand slowness. Instead, He is patient with you, not wanting anyone to perish, but for everyone to come to repentance." —2 Peter 3:9

How many of us have asked the question, "Why does healing take so long?" Having been on my own personal journey of healing for over forty-five years, I've asked it many times. When I was being trained as an RTF minister almost fifteen years ago, I was having some personal ministry and asked my ministers, "Why has it taken almost forty years to find this healing?" As Betsy Kylstra prayed, she heard the Lord say, *"Because there was no one safe enough to help you."*

I had been through hundreds of counseling sessions and various ministries over the years but had only made minimal progress in certain areas of personal healing. When I got close to the darkest parts of my heart, where the wounding was most severe, I would often experience a judgment from the minister that would shut it down and close off my heart once again. I heard things like, *"How dare you have those thoughts! You blasphemer you!"* You get the picture. My pain would trigger something in them that they couldn't handle.

After many years of doing RTF ministry, God gave me a deeper understanding of why some healing takes longer than others; that it was part of His plan. He said to me it is like the parable of the wheat and the tares (Matt 13:24–30). You remember the story, about how the farmer had planted a new crop of good seed, but in the night his enemy came and planted weeds in among the good seed. When the weeds and good seeds started sprouting together and the servants saw the weeds, they asked the farmer, *"Do you want us to go and pull them up?"* But the owner's response was probably not what they expected when he said, *"No! When you are pulling up the weeds, you may pull up the wheat!"* (The wheat is the good seed.) He told them to wait until the plants were full grown, then separate the weeds from the wheat, and to burn the weeds.

What God was saying to me in this was that the good seed He has planted in each of our hearts is so precious to Him that He doesn't want any damage done to a single seed. It is out of His goodness and His valuing of the good seed within us that the process of healing takes as long as it takes. Each of us has a unique journey to finish that work, even if it takes a lifetime.

This word has been a comfort to me and to many we have ministered to on this journey. It was so freeing to me as a minister, knowing that I could trust God's timing and that each person would receive as much healing as they were ready for and that God said they were ready for. Hallelujah! It frees me up from my performance issues or any sense of personal failure if God doesn't show up and give them all their healing right then. It is definitely a process; and that is a good thing! I've never been fond of "process" healing, but it is often the way God does His best work in us. I'm learning to trust and rest in that truth.

This is not a cop out or a "quick fix" answer for why healing doesn't happen at any given moment. And it certainly doesn't stop us from praying for people's healing and believing for divine supernatural healings. But it does give us a glimpse into why God's ways are *"so much higher than man's ways"* and are ultimately the best way to *"finish the good work I've begun in you!"* (Phil 1:6).

I hope you will be encouraged by this as I was, knowing that God is responsible for the healing and I am only responsible to do my part. I believe we call this a "boundary" definition, knowing my part, God's part, and the receiver's part. May you be blessed as you press in for more of Him and the fullness of your healing until we are all made complete in Him.

Revelation #12: *The "Issue" Is never the issue!*

"For my ways are not your ways. My ways are so much higher than your ways..." —Isaiah 55:8–9

Last night, I felt like the Lord was bringing me more revelation about so many of me and my wife's issues. I felt like He was saying that the issue at hand or the problem I was wrestling with was never the real issue. The issue is not about my financial problems, the issue is not about my relationship problems, the issue is not about my addiction or anger issues; the issue is always just a prelude or an opportunity to draw me nearer to God, to bring me into His presence, or to train me how to be in His presence. And as I am in His presence, I am changed, and the issue is no longer the issue.

Some of you might "take issue" with this, but I recommend you take it up with Him and see what He says.

CHAPTER 4

HOLY SPIRIT!

Revelation #13: *God's "Glory Bubble" is MY safe place!*

"I pray that out of His glorious riches He may strengthen you with power through His Spirit in your inner being." –Ephesians 3:16

T his past weekend, I officiated my first wedding in almost seventeen years. I did several when I was pastoring twenty-five years ago but none since. It was a joyous time, and I felt blessed to walk in my anointing as a pastor. In preparing the wedding address for the service, the Lord gave me a great picture to help me focus the multitude of pages I had about weddings and marriage and intimacy and other related subjects.

He reminded me of a teaching that Mahesh Chavda had shared five years before at All Nations Church (where they just happen to go to church currently) that was about "stepping into God's glory bubble." God was saying He had a special glory bubble for them as a new couple. It was a place of protection, power, peace, provision, and the very presence of Himself! If they chose to live in His glory bubble, the enemy was powerless to steal their peace or prevent God's divine purposes for their lives. It is the place where true intimacy can happen, where they can truly be "naked and unashamed," which is His heart for us, to restore us back to that place of closeness with Him and each other.

God was very present at this holy and sacred time, and during their vows, two doves landed on the branches above the gazebo where we were having the ceremony. God made Himself clearly known and felt.

I was also invited to bring an address to the RTF students as they started their training at Echo Mountain Inn the next day. As I was preparing, God said this same concept would be important for them as they walked through the challenges of their schooling. God showed me that He wanted to give us this glory bubble in place of all the walls we've built and the fortress of our own self-protection that the enemy has helped us build.

It was so cool to see the Lord show this contrast between what He offers us and what the enemy offers us (and which we tend to accept and walk in). For me, the picture and concept seemed very do-able and that I could envision myself stepping into that place of glory. The cool thing is, that glory bubble goes with us wherever we go, and just like the hula-hoop of our personal boundaries, no one is permitted in unless He allows it!

Overall, it was an awesome weekend. The Lord was reaffirming me as a pastor and all the joys and authority that go with that mantle. I thank Him for this encouragement, and I'm excited about what He is bringing forth in my life.

Revelation #14: *Spiritual Warfare is a NORMAL part of being a disciple of Christ.*

"And these signs shall follow them that believe: in my name they will drive out demons; they will speak with new tongues; they will pick up snakes with their hands; and when they drink deadly poison, it will not hurt them at all; they will place their hands on sick people, and they will get well."
—Mark 16:17–18

While there is great controversy around demons and spiritual warfare, the truth remains that God says in His Word that demons are real, and that it is our appointed task to get rid of them, along with other spiritual disciplines.

In RTF ministry, one of the core areas we address is demonic oppression and removing the legal ground for it to be there. While we cannot be possessed by demons as believers, we can be oppressed. God has lots to say in the scripture about demons and warfare. In Ephesians 6, He tells us that our *"battle is NOT against flesh and blood, but against the principalities and powers of this dark world."* In James 5, He says, *"Submit to God, Resist the Devil, and he will flee from you!"* And in Ephesians 6, He tells us about putting on the Armor of God, *"that we might resist the fiery darts of the evil one."* Why is it so hard to believe that we are in a spiritual battle and that we need to learn how to do spiritual warfare?

About a year after we had been doing RTF ministry, while doing the demonic oppression session, God gave me a vision of a huge neon sign behind the receiver that read, "NORMAL!!!" He showed me that doing deliverance was just a normal part of being a disciple of Jesus Christ; that this was the job assignment for every believer in Jesus. This is one of the first things He did on earth with His disciples.

Remember how He had sent them out two by two to bring the gospel and healing to all who would hear? When they returned, they were all excited and said to Jesus, *"Even the devils obey us,"* which Jesus followed up with, *"Don't be glad that the devils obey you, but rather be grateful that your name is written in the Lamb's book of life." (Luke 10:17-20)* Jesus didn't want them to be prideful about the power they carried but that their very life and salvation was a gift from their Heavenly Father. After all, Jesus did say that we would *"do even greater things than I have done"* (Jn 14:12).

We don't have to be super spiritual giants, religious zealots, or an exorcist of some kind. Just any ordinary believer will do—even children. He is inviting us to step up to the plate and be His disciple, with all that it entails. It is exciting to know that He has already *defeated* and *disarmed* the enemy, *"publicly humiliating them by Jesus on the Cross"* (Col 2). In other words, Satan has zero legitimate authority and power. He only has what he can steal from us through trickery and deception. WE have the legitimate power and authority, and he wants to use our authority to release his agenda. When we do spiritual warfare, we are just being your average, normal, obedient disciple of Jesus Christ. What's so difficult about that? Let's all sharpen our swords and take back all that the enemy has stolen. The victory is already ours!

Revelation #15: *WHO you listen to makes ALL the difference –*
opinion vs. truth

"A fool takes no pleasure in understanding, but only
in expressing his opinion." —Proverbs 18:2

Back in seminary, which seems a few lifetimes ago, we were taught to do tons of research and study in preparation for our sermons and teachings. Even when preparing for my first sermon on Romans 12:1–2 that I did at the age of twenty, I read at least six commentaries as part of my preparation.

As I became a pastor, it was very important and even prestigious to have read or owned many volumes of books. I enjoyed reading, so it was easy to fall in line with this thinking. Over the years I accumulated thousands of books, even inheriting two other pastors' libraries. I was very proud of my book collection. I would spend a minimum of twenty hours a week reading these men's opinions in preparation for my twenty-minute sermons and really believed I was being diligent and faithful by preparing this way. I learned some Greek and Hebrew and how to parse words, from present active infinitive to past present accusative, to infinity and beyond.

And I was a pretty good preacher, I thought. I knew to add cartoons, poems, catchy stories, and make my three points. But God had a different plan for me.

After my meltdown in '97 and loss of marriage, loss of church, loss of faith, loss of income, loss of retirement, and loss of home and car, I still at least had my books! Until one day on my journey of healing, God spoke to me about my books, *"Son, I want you to stop listening to everyone else's opinion and start listening to Me!"*

This meant I needed to go directly to the source, to read the Word and listen to the Holy Spirit for God's truth, and to get rid of most of my library of men's opinions. "Are you kidding? How do I do that?" I thought. Do you ever feel like you would like to hold on to at least one thing of your own that can just be yours? Well this was a big one for me. This was just one more of my control issues He was working on.

When I sold or got rid of 90 percent of my books, I started hearing Him more clearly. I started learning about "hearing the voice of God", as taught by Mark Virkler and others. I heard Him in Theophostic ministry, RTF ministry, and other ministry times. I heard Him reading the Word and journaling, and I even heard Him just while walking and talking. His thoughts, His voice, and His truth began to take precedence over all the other opinions that had been swirling around my brain for decades. He started connecting the dots, using all that I had learned over the years. He doesn't let anything go to waste!

I'll never forget the morning after finishing my fifteen-hour thorough RTF ministry. After waking up, my mind was completely quiet. For the first time in over twenty years (or at least as long as I could remember), I was at peace and completely quiet inside, without all the questions and discussions and plans and strategizing, and so forth. It was almost shocking. Since then I have been learning who to listen to and who to tell to shut up and leave! Who we listen to and who influences our thinking is a significant part of walking out our healing, impacting our ability to quickly recognize and embrace the truth.

The mocker loves to bring his judgments and criticisms and to help us interpret his version of what God must mean. He did it right there in the garden of Eden, when after God had clearly said to Adam and Eve, *"You must not eat of the tree of the knowledge of good and evil, for when you eat of it you will surely die"*(Gen 2:17), Satan said, *"Surely you will <u>not</u> die! But you will become like God."* We need to know the real Word of God, the living Word of God, Jesus, in order to be able to interpret the written Word. I am much more selective now about what I read and always need to weigh it against His Word, and what His Spirit speaks to my heart about it.

Getting rid of most of my books was a good thing. Though books can be an important and valuable way to learn what God has revealed to others, He alone is ultimately the source and filter through which everything we read must be considered. I am grateful for the *"many counselors"* I have had over the years and currently have, but I'm especially glad that Jesus sent the Holy Spirit to be our true guide to leads us to *"the truth that sets us free!"* (Jn 8:31–32).

Always consider the source, and don't be afraid to check it out. There are false prophets and false spirits that want to deceive and destroy. (Matt 24:23-27; 2 Pet 3:3; Jud 17–18) God is not intimidated by our questions but loves it when we are wise in the searching out of His truths. *"It is the glory of God to conceal a matter; to search out a matter is the glory of Kings!"* (Prov. 25:2). You and I are royalty, and it is our job and our delight to search out His most precious truths. Ask, seek, and knock are not a parable, but a divine directive. Enjoy the treasure hunt and celebrate the joy of discovery.

Revelation #16: *Identifying the Mocker can save your life.*

> *"Now have come salvation, strength, the kingdom of our God, and the power of His Christ. For the accuser of the brethren has been cast down, who accused us before God day and night. And they overcame him by the blood of the lamb and the word of their testimony."*—Revelation 12:11

When I first learned about this scripture, it was in the context of working through addiction and temptation, learning how to resist the enemy. Later, after hearing many people talk about how they were too shameful or dirty to go to God, it dawned on me, that if the most-evil creature who hates God can be in His presence, why can't I?

About six years ago, God began showing us more about the role of the mocker, this *"accuser of the brethren,"* and how he was affecting relationships. The mocker doesn't just accuse us before God, he accuses God before us. He accuses spouses to each other, children to their parents, the pastor to the parishioner, the boss to the worker, siblings to siblings, and so forth. Get the picture? God was highlighting how much the accuser or mocker was mocking or belittling us to each other—and we often believe him. He did it right there in the Garden of Eden, mocking God to Adam and Eve, contradicting Gods' words blatantly; and they fell for it.

The mocker has been very active in our lives and relationships, planting lies and ungodly beliefs about each other. In my last revelation, "Who you listen to makes all the difference" (#15), I was talking primarily about listening to other men. But today, I want to turn the focus on Satan, the enemy of our soul, whose primary desire is to *"steal, kill, and destroy!"* (Jn 10:10).

Having done individual ministry with almost a thousand people, we have noticed that many of the conflicts and misunderstandings people experience have come because they listened to the enemy's accusations against one another, themselves, or God. The results have been devastating to their relationships. It's like the control-rebellion-rejection stronghold and how the enemy starts a fight between people and sits back and laughs as couples react and wound each other.

Paul says in Ephesians 6, *"Your enemy is NOT against flesh and blood, but against the principalities and powers of this dark world."* We often remind couples that their spouse is NOT their enemy. The mocker is the one accusing them to one another, and they need to put a stop to it. One of the scriptures I find encouraging in this battle is Colossians 2:13–15, which talks about how Jesus *"disarmed the powers and authorities, making a public spectacle of them, defeating them at the cross."* In other words, the enemy has zero legitimate authority. He only has what he can trick us into giving him.

We have true legitimate authority and power, given to us by God through our relationship with Jesus Christ. It is our job to pay attention to who we are listening to, to deny the mocker's voice, and to give him a black eye! A picture we like using when we are doing deliverance is picturing the demon as a little ant who sits on your shoulder and says, "Put your dukes up!" God says to simply flick him off. God has given us legitimate and ultimate authority over the enemy's schemes and strategies.

"The weapons we fight with are not the weapons of the world. On the contrary, we have divine power to demolish strongholds. We demolish arguments and every pretension that sets itself up against the knowledge of God, and we take captive every though to make it obedient to Christ."
—2 Corinthians 10:14–15

Next time you are hearing some critical thoughts about yourself, your authorities, your spouse, your kids, or even God, take a moment and see who you are listening to. Know your authority and activate it by telling the mocker to shut up and get out. And see the deliverance of the Lord. Even the rebellious demons who don't want to go, I turn them over to the Lord Jesus Christ and watch them scatter!

Jesus gives His disciples this power and authority, which we rejoice in. But as He said to His disciples, *"Don't rejoice that the demons obey you, but rejoice that your names are written in the Lamb's book of life"* (Luke 10:19–20). Jesus is faithful to help us keep our lives in balance. I celebrate these gifts and pray you will be able to activate them in your lives as you see the deliverance of the Lord.

CHAPTER 5

BODY OF CHRIST

Revelation #17: God has a personal assignment just for me.
–Part 1"

"From Him the whole body, joined and held together by every supporting ligament, grows and builds itself up in love, as each part does its work."
–Ephesians 4:16

G od and I were having a discussion recently about why I felt like I hadn't been able to experience any physical miracles of my own. My faith for them was there; I've seen many of them, and I've even seen some when praying with Linda. I know that healed marriages and hearts and emotions and relationships are all miracles, which I celebrate and give thanks for, but I still hadn't seen any direct result of my prayers releasing God's miracle of physical healing in that moment. The enemy tries to harass me in this area sometimes, trying to get me to doubt myself or my calling. I do spiritual warfare on a regular basis, but it still bothered me.

As I was talking with God about this, I felt He was trying to help me process through to something deeper. He reminded me that we are not all called to do the same thing, including having an anointing for physical miracles. He drew my attention to I Corinthians 12–14 and reminded me that even though the gifts are important, they're not the end goal. I could raise someone from the dead, but it wouldn't mean anything without love. He reminded me that I was built for love and that my greatest gift is the ability to love. In the end, the gifts themselves will disappear and all that remains will be His love. I know this is true, but something in me wants more physical demonstration of His power and presence, perhaps just to prove that my faith is real and that my life will mean something.

About eighteen years ago, when I was working at the Coliseum in Portland at a Rolling Stones concert, I was watching some Christians arguing with a man about how sinful it was for him to come to this concert, and I so wanted to go over and run them off and give them a piece of my righteous mind. God clearly said, *"Don't go. You are not ready for this. I've not called you to that assignment."* I knew He was right, but it made me feel sad and a little hurt, even though He was gentle in His correction and direction. That's how I felt when He said I wasn't necessarily called to have an anointing for physical healing but that my calling was just as important, if not even more significant, than having a physical healing anointing. It felt a little like when He told me I was called to "*the One*" and not the ninety-nine. I had believed I wasn't good enough or spiritual enough or believing enough to accomplish a miracle like that.

Perhaps He's just protecting me from pride or from wanting to bolster my own sense of self-worth by being viewed as a miracle-worker. I know I have the belief for it. I know we are called to take hold of our inheritance and call down divine gifts from Heaven. But I was wrestling with the thought that I still wasn't doing enough by just loving people and helping them come to a place of healing and wholeness with Him.

Perhaps this is where a lot of us find ourselves when it comes to seeing or not seeing healing miracles, believing more spiritual people can do it but we can't. The tendency to compare and judge ourselves based on this ability or not can be very disheartening and even cause us to question our faith, wondering if God is really using us at all.

Perhaps a deeper lesson in this for me is to know my specific assignment from Him and to be faithful and obedient to walk in that divine assignment without looking at what others are doing. We talk a lot about "divine appointments" and How God sets them up for us when we are willing to let Him lead. I know He talks about the body of Christ and each having a different part, and that one part shouldn't be jealous of another part that looks more important (Eph 4), but we still struggle sometimes looking at what others have and we don't!

This is a humbling lesson for me, and though there may even be others jealous of my gifting as a pastor or teacher or singer, I need to rejoice in the assignments He has for me, trusting that it will be fulfilling and satisfying. In the end, we all need each other, and the body needs each of us to do his/her specific part for the whole Body to be healthy and productive.

I will continue to pray for people's physical healing, along with their spiritual and emotional healing, trusting that God is doing a supernatural work in their lives and that He deserves all the credit for every good thing that comes forth. I choose to look for His assignments and only His. Regardless of my doubts and fears, I choose to trust His love for me and that it's all going to be worth it in the end. Thank you, Lord!

Revelation #18: God has a personal assignment just for me. –Part 2"

King David's greatest desire was to build a temple for the Lord. But for various reasons, he was not given permission to accomplish that task. After he died, his son Solomon was the one to complete his dream. In I Kings 8:18, when David's son, Solomon, was dedicating the temple of the Lord, God spoke to him and said, *"You did well to have it in your heart to build a temple for my name" (NIV); "You wanted to build the temple to honor my name. Your intention is good" (NLT); "Whereas, it was in thine heart to build a house unto my Name, thou didst well that it was in thine heart" (KJV).*

A Key lesson here is that God honors us for what is in our hearts, NOT just what we can accomplish or achieve with our actions.

I heard this preached thirty-five years ago, and it has remained with me as one of the most profound truths. It has encouraged and sustained me, especially when I haven't been able to see the fruit or accomplishments I had hoped for in my life. It has always been in my heart to do great things for my Lord, to courageously follow His leading, and to trust Him with all my heart. However, I have often felt I fell short of the mark, did not measure up, and was cowardly and timid in stepping out for my faith. I needed to be in control of things, to protect myself, and constantly argued with Him or wrestled with Him about what or how things should be. I had to know things in order to feel secure. I just didn't seem to know how to completely trust Him or trust that He wanted only the very best for me.

I often joked I was truly a *"son of Jacob,"* my name being Jacobson, that I was one to always *"wrestle with God."*

The reason I bring this up is what I was just writing about in my previous revelation about how I questioned whether God was using me, asking why I was not able to witness a miracle of physical healing when I prayed for someone while others did. I can see now that there are some ungodly beliefs here that have brought torment to my heart and caused me to question my faith and God's faith in me. It is too easy to look at others and what they are accomplishing but I am not. Then the mocker tells me I don't measure up, that I am failing somehow, that I could never do what they are doing, and so forth.

The truth God is reminding me of is that He always looks at our heart. And it is from the heart that all things flow, including His heart for us, which is always unconditionally loving, gracious, and wanting the best for us. Once again, I'm reminded to keep my eyes on Him and off the consequences or results of something. I need to be obedient to His leading for each assignment and trust the outcome to Him.

I'm grateful that He cares more about my heart than my performance and that He honors me for my heart's desires. It brings me much comfort and hope. Even though there is still a little pain sometimes, there is an even greater joy in knowing that His love and discipline are real, powerful, and life changing.

REVELATION #19: *"The REAL church of Christ: Organization vs. Organism*

"I will build MY church…" –Matthew 16:18

Recently, we'd been talking about what to call our new house-church or fellowship. I felt prompted to do a little Bible study and see what it says about church. As I read a few passages about church in the Bible, one consistent pattern arose: *Christ is the head of the church* (Col 1:24 & Eph. 5:23). He calls it *"My"* church (Matt 16:18); and in Acts 20:28, it says, *"Be shepherds of the CHURCH of God, which He bought with HIS own blood."* And in Ephesians 4:4&13, it talks about the *"Body of Christ,"* which means His church.

Last week, in John Eldredge's Ransomed Heart daily reading, he wrote a little article about the church, which I felt had some key truths in this discussion. In it, he referred to some wisdom from Brother Andrew. "Church is not a building. It is not an event that takes place on Sundays. When Scripture talks about church, it means community, the little fellowships of the heart that are outposts of the kingdom. A shared life" (see Acts 12:12). He compared churches to army platoons, where men and women fight bravely for each other, where there is true heroism, sacrifice, and devotion; that devotion takes place in small units, just like a family.

A chaplain friend of mine who helped me through some of my healing shared that the <u>true church is an organism, not an organization</u>. An organism is "a living and spontaneous association of individuals who know one another intimately, care for each other deeply, and feel a kind of respect for one another that makes rules and bylaws unnecessary." An organization is a man-made, man-directed structure of rules to control a group of people. John concluded his reading with this thought, "I'm simply helping you accept reality—that whatever else you do, you must have a small fellowship to walk with you and fight with you and bandage your wounds. This is essential!"

Although I have experienced some of this kind of church, I have also encountered the church that "shoots their walking wounded." Part of my story was experiencing being removed as a pastor, after my ex-wife had left and asked for a divorce. It left me deeply wounded and confused about who I was as a believer and who I was as a pastor. When the church's response was to dismiss me without any support, counsel, or assistance, I was left with a bitter taste in my mouth. It would be the first of four bitter betrayals and rejections by organizations. Is it any surprise I had an aversion to wanting to start a church or to call our gathering a "church"?

As I was preparing to preach on Easter in Raleigh, North Carolina, God got a hold of me in a big way. I was teaching about death and resurrection cycles, and asking the question, "Are we willing to lay down our hopes and dreams, along with our hurts and wounds, at the foot of the cross, and allow Him to either resurrect the dreams or replace the bad with the good in our lives?" While preparing this sermon and studying about the church at the same time, I realized I was ashamed of the church! And if I was ashamed of the church, I was ashamed of Jesus. That really gripped my heart.

As I was sharing this on Easter, preparing myself to lay down some things at the cross, I heard Him say, *"Why are you resisting picking up the gift I gave you thirty years ago?"* I had resisted going back into anything that looked like pastor in any official capacity. Perhaps I was hiding behind the role of counselor and teacher and deliverance minister the past fifteen years. On Easter morning 2015, I made a pubic confession that I would embrace and activate my calling as a pastor. This was even before I laid down the other stuff at the cross. I was able to reaffirm something He had told me years ago, *"Pastoring isn't what you do, it is who you are!"*

Resurrection day was indeed a personal resurrection for me! Only this time, I was laying down my judgments, my shame, my resistance and self-will, and picking up my true calling and gifting, along with a heart full of gratitude. God is healing the hurts, and my experiences from the past are now part of my "credentials." He has taken *"what the enemy meant for evil and turned it into something good (of eternal value)."* HALLELUJAH! Though I am still a *"work in progress,"* I am choosing to embrace my calling and the journey He has for me.

It was a joy to see the response of the congregation and to see them activate their faith, as they all laid down hopes, dreams, hurts, and wounds at the foot of the cross and stepped into a bright new future with resurrected hopes and dreams and new beginnings. To me, they were being the church, and I was genuinely grateful to be part of this incredible family who loved Jesus! (If you want to hear Brian's Easter message, you can watch it at this podcast: http://www.newbethelnc.org/podcasts.)

Revelation #20: *The Re-Birthing of His Church is an ongoing activity.*

God is doing something new for Linda and me. We are excitedly anticipating the birth of a new church, which we have already named "HIS Heart2Heart Fellowship!" We were watching a Joyce Meyer teaching a while back, and she was talking about the birthing of new ministries. She brought several pregnant women up on stage who were at different stages of pregnancy; to demonstrate the different stages of the birthing process. We felt like God was saying we are in a birthing process and that at that time we were in the first trimester of the process. In Joyce Meyer's amplified version of Genesis 1:1, it says, *"In the Beginning God* (prepared, formed, fashioned) *created the heavens and the earth"*; and in Hebrews 11:3, *"By faith we understand that the worlds*

were framed (fashioned, put in order, and equipped for their intended purpose) *by the Word of God so that what we see is not made out of things which are visible."*

Linda got the original vision for this five years ago, followed a year later by the words *"planning, preparation, and provision,"* which really line up with what God is now doing. I was a bit slower to get on board. God has been working on me. When I had the opportunity to do a wedding in January (the first one in seventeen years), it really sparked in me a new excitement and joy of being a father and pastor again. And now, it is starting to look like a reality. In addition to that, at Easter I preached in Raleigh, North Carolina, and they asked us to be "Fathers/Mothers" of the church because of the work we had done in pouring healing into so many in that community. What an honor and a joy!

The key focus of this new ministry is to truly be an RTF church, to live out of the mandate from Isaiah 61, to restore, rebuild, and renew, and also to release. Not only have we missed not having regular fellowship and worship, but we also know there is such a need for true discipleship, to retrain the body of Christ about what it means to be His disciples!

When we were praying about what to name our ministry, some voiced they didn't want to call it a "church". In the past, I would have wholeheartedly agreed. And while the name "church" isn't in the title, we are choosing to recognize our fellowship as His church, His body, His work. And we are grateful to call ourselves His children.

We welcome your prayers as we embark on this new adventure. We will continue to be RTF ministers, with a focus on healing and deliverance. But our role is expanding into more discipleship and teaching of all that He has taught us. Thanks for being with us on this journey together with the King of Kings and Lord of Lords. What a ride.

Revelation #21: *God is divinely re-defining the purpose of the current church to make it relevant.*

> *"Now you are the body of Christ, and each one of you is a part of it."* —I Corinthians 12:27

As I was asking the Lord about His leading us to start an RTF church, I heard, "*You are the church.*" I thought about it further and started exploring and listening to what that meant. The church is not a location, a building, a place, an organization; It is you, it is the manifest presence of Jesus; it is *"where two or three are gathered in His name"*; it is where love is being enacted; it is in my kingdom DNA; it is the spiritual reality of God's presence wherever it is found on the earth, where Jesus is present and Lord; it is where the kingdom of God is realized; it is a who.

We have for too long thought of the church as a building, or at least an organization, where people gather to worship and have a service or ritual, where people meet for fellowship with a common belief system.

In truth, the Church is a living organism, where each living part is interconnected and interdependent on the others for health, life, and purpose, directed by one Head, who is Jesus.

HOW can one recognize the church? The church is where there is the love of the Father, the worship of Jesus as Lord, the fruit and presence of the Holy Spirit. It doesn't just happen on Sunday or Wednesday or at a meeting in a building. It happens whenever one heart touches another with the love of God; it happens when one life is changed by the prayers of another; it happens when two believers come in agreement and unity and humility; it happens whenever we have fellowship with Jesus, anytime, anywhere. It takes place in time and outside of time, on the earth and in heavenly places; it goes wherever you go. It has no limitations, but it has boundaries and is defined by Heavenly Father; it is about order, not chaos; it is about people's hearts, not performance; it is a work of grace, not of good works, *"lest any man should boast"* (Rom).

The church is built on and made up of people, with Jesus as the cornerstone, *upon whom the whole body is built up.* It is in the heart of every believer to beat with the same rhythm of the Lord, to be in sync, and to share His lifeblood, His eternal life, His purity and righteousness, His authority and power, as well as His love and unity with the Father. The church is meant to be the bride of Christ; and when they are wed, they will become one, as Ephesians 4 talks about. The church is *"Bought and paid for."*

The church is about location only when the Spirit of God is welcomed, present, and ruling, in the people and on the earth.

When God asked us to start an RTF church, what was He really asking? He said it wouldn't look like anything we'd seen before. I said to Him that I didn't want to do *"church as usual."* Is it possible that He has already begun an RTF church? He said we would do all that He did on the earth, and even more.

Isn't every touch, every word, every act of love and kindness, every prayer, every choice to follow Him, every heart being changed, every thought towards Him, the church?

RTF is all about *"preparing the bride for the bridegroom."* The church is inside every one of His children, and God wants it to be set free. The Church is about life and restoration, not death; the Church is about forgiveness and freedom, not about control and judgment; the Church is about embracing the truth; *"Jesus IS the way, the truth, and the life"* (Isa 53:6; Rom 5). If we are a disciple of Christ, are we not the church? *"If we obey His commands, we are truly His disciples; and we will know the truth, and the truth will set us free"* (Jn 8). The church is when and where we have divine exchanges. Whenever a transfer of love happens, church happens; whenever a heart is touched or changed, church happens; whenever there is fellowship in the Spirit, church happens!

It's interesting that when someone becomes a new believer, one of the first things said to them is that they need to "find a church" or "go to church" as part of their follow through as a new Christian. In truth, they just found Church—with Jesus! Now He wants them to learn how to grow in that understanding with other believers, in loving relationship and discipleship. We often think the new believer just needs to go to all the meetings and become just like the rest of the church crowd. God wants new believers to encounter the encouragement and love of a true fellowship of worshipers of Christ; to be built up, comforted, healed, and empowered with Kingdom values and gifts; to know their true place as "first born sons/daughters of the King."

Church is meant to be foremost, a family of faith.

What has been your experience with the church? Have you encountered it lately? Where can you go to find this exchange? Maybe you're already doing "church" and don't even know it. Are the signs there? What does your heart tell you? Do you see the fruit of the Spirit present? Do you see the signs of love present? Do you see the power of healing and the peace of God's Spirit? All we need do is *"Ask, seek, and knock,"* and we will know the truth.

CHAPTER 6

LIFE LESSONS

Revelation #22: *Revelation: the Verb*

"The Revelation of Jesus Christ...blessed are those who HEAR it and take it to heart...because the time is near." —Revelation 1:1–3

I find it interesting how often I hear people refer to the last book in the Bible as the Book of Revelations, not Revelation. The book starts with Jesus Christ and ends with Jesus Christ. It's not a book of information but revelation, which means it is personal, a new discovery, an ongoing revealing of the person of Jesus Christ, who is the Alpha and the Omega, the *"First and the last; I am the Living one; I was dead, and behold I am alive forever and ever. And I hold the keys of death and Hades"* (Rev 1:18).

In this book, Jesus has a message for His Church, which He sees as *urgent and imminent.* He goes on to address these seven churches very specifically, pointing out their strengths and weaknesses. In every case He says to them, *"He who has an ear, let him hear what the Spirit says to the churches"* (Rev 2:7, 11, 17, 29; 3:6, 13, 22).

In addition to this command, He offers a promise: to each church is given a specific blessing that begins with the words, *"He who overcomes . . ."* (Rev 2 & 3), "he who *presses in*, who *seeks out*, who *endures*, who *obeys and follows His leading*," and so forth. This is the verb aspect of revelation. It is a journey of discovery, an "ask, seek, and knock" kind of thing, a relational knowing that comes with hanging out with Jesus. In other words, it is an active, ever-present, continual, and ongoing activity of getting to know our Lord and savior, Jesus Christ. And He sees this as urgent and essential.

It seems there are always discussions about Jesus' return, and I often hear people say it is "near and imminent" and that the signs prove it must be soon. Of course, there are many days I would like that too, especially if it means I don't have to go through any more painful stuff here on earth but could be translated to heaven right now. I can't seem to get beyond the words that Jesus himself said, that *"no one knows about that day or hour, not even the angels in heaven, nor the Son, but only the Father"* (Matt 24:36). In Acts 1:7, Jesus addresses the curiosity of the disciples: *"It is not for you to know the times or dates the Father has set by His own authority."*

This says to me I'm not supposed to get hung up on or obsessed with knowing the exact time of His coming, to live in a state of readiness not fear. The language of imminence by Jesus in the Book of Revelation is undeniable. He spoke those words over 2000 years ago, so did He get it wrong? What was so urgent? Why did He say He was coming soon? Why did He say to the man on the cross, *"Today you will be with me in paradise..."? (Luke 23:43)* What we have learned about God, that He can walk outside of time, puts a whole new slant on what this scripture means.

When we look for knowledge about Jesus, it will always be one dimensional, limited, and incomplete. However, when we seek to know the *living* Jesus, who He is continuously revealing Himself to be, He is always willing to clearly show Himself and His heart for us. In fact, He invites us into that kind of relationship in Revelation 3:20, *"Here I am! I stand at the door and knock. If anyone HEARS my voice and opens the door, I will come in and eat with him, and he with me"* (NIV).

He seems to be loudly saying that we need to clearly hear Him, to be listening and paying attention to what He is saying. Much of religion tells us that God doesn't speak to us or is hard to hear. Really? If we can't hear Him, then how can we know what He is trying to say, or what He is asking us to do? How can we possibly understand His specific leading and mentoring of us if we are in the dark? I believe this is possibly the linchpin that unlocks the secret of His revelation. Do you have the key?

I am always impressed with how Jesus leads by invitation rather than command, when it comes to us, His children. This is where He meets us every day, knocking at the door of our hearts, seeing if we are listening for His voice, waiting to see if we will open up and let Him come to be with us in whatever we are doing. He says in John that *"My sheep know my voice."* He's not trying to keep Himself hidden or make it difficult for us to hear Him.

The only one telling us that Jesus doesn't talk to us or want to be with us or doesn't love us is His archenemy, the spirit of the Antichrist. It is this spirit that often uses us as unwitting instruments to curse one another and to keep us from hearing our Lord or even wanting to hear Him. This is the spirit we need to reject and oppose. (see Isa 54:17)

"What's the Lord saying to you today?" is a question we ask all the time. And most people seem perplexed that we would ask such a ridiculous question. Isn't it interesting how popular it is for many Christians to walk around today with the bracelet, WWJD (what would Jesus do?), but don't even believe that they can hear Him? How much crazier would it be if we asked, *"What is the Lord REVEALING to you today?"* Yet I believe this is more the question we NEED to be asking! And then SHARING with one another His answers!

As the body of Christ, the Church, we are in urgent need of hearing the voice of God, more than ever before. It is the question of the day. And it starts with a 'yes' to His invitation to listen, to ask, to seek, to observe, to learn, to be His disciple, and to obey His commands. This leads us to truth, which leads us to freedom. And it's an amazing journey. Enjoy the Ride.

If you have any questions about this, feel free to let me know. But more importantly, ask Him, the source of all life. Jesus says at the end of the Book of Revelation, *"I am coming soon!* (Rev 22). Folks, He is already here! Thank you, Lord, for being here. Amen and Amen.

Revelation #23: *Rejection: a Matter of Perspective*

"He was despised and rejected by men, a man of sorrows, acquainted with grief." —Isaiah 53:3

Rejection is one of the core wounds that many of us experience in life, which often feeds what we call the "orphan lifestyle" or "orphan thinking." Many of us are familiar with this terminology and may know some of the characteristics such as abandonment, neglect, independent thinking, anger, mistrust, fatherlessness, restlessness, hypervigilance, and so forth.

Rejection is often associated with the shame-fear-control demonic stronghold that is taught in RTF. It is also a part of the control-rejection-rebellion stronghold, which feeds the destruction of intimacy and relationships. In other words, it is a very destructive force that seems to play a major part in many of our lives. But how did Jesus handle His rejection? Did He act like an orphan? Did He choose to respond in these ways? How was He able to choose something differently when He faced rejection?

In my own life, I've experienced many rejections on many levels. When my father left our family when I was six, I felt rejected and abandoned. When I wasn't chosen for the basketball team, I felt rejected. When I went through my divorce, I felt rejected and ashamed. When the pastor of my church decided to usurp all authority and shut down the church, I felt rejected and victimized. And when I was kicked out of the Free Methodist church as a pastor, I felt rejected, crushed, and thrown away like trash. It is this last experience I want to share about that God brought me some new revelation that set me free from some of the sting and trauma of rejection.

After serving as a Methodist pastor for about five years, I was being prepared to be ordained as a deacon. However, other things were about to take place. My wife at the time was unhappy as a pastor's wife, along with many other issues. This led to her deciding to leave one weekend when I was away at a pastors' conference. We tried to resolve our issues but to no avail. The denomination's response to my separation was ultimately to let me go as a pastor without any support or assistance. It was all a crushing blow. It felt like one rejection after another. I had no idea how God could possibly restore or heal the level of devastation I was experiencing at that dark time of my life.

Over the next seven years of healing, forgiving, and restoring, God began to reframe how I saw this experience. He began to reframe my life, my belief system, and ultimately my future. As I walked through His process of healing my broken life, He took the belief that I was "thrown away" and reframed it into the truth that I was "delivered"! He showed me that if I had stayed under that religious system of oppression and legalism it would have been death to my spirit. He showed me that He had removed me from that system and brought not only personal healing, but a new outlook on who I was and who I could become as His child.

He was taking me from an orphan lifestyle to that of true sonship. He knew that I needed more healing and that I wouldn't find it where I was at. I remember asking Betsy Kylstra once why this healing had taken so long, and the Holy Spirit said to her, "*Because there wasn't anyone safe enough.*" This motivates me to want to be that safe person for others, to be a person that will help set them free.

God showed me He was always there with me through this journey of rejection, sorrow, hurt, and pain. He, too, knew what it was like to experience such suffering and sorrow. At one point in my journey, Jesus came to me and asked me for MY forgiveness for all the hurt and suffering. It was extremely humbling. He demonstrated to me His character of humility, which I'd never really understood before.

I've experienced the pain of being "thrown away" several times since then but now understand it as God moving me to another level of healing, and even anointing, for His intended purposes for my life. While I can't say that I'll ever enjoy the experience of "rejection," I know that He can reframe it and give it purpose as He heals my heart. He showed me that rejection is a matter of perspective. Consider Jesus' perspective: *"For the joy set before Him, He endured the Cross, scorning its shame... Consider Him who endured such opposition from sinful men, so that you will not grow weary and lose heart"* (Heb 12:2–3).

While I may have felt rejected, or encountered the rejection of others, it doesn't mean that I am rejected. It is not my identity, and it does not have to determine whether I have peace and joy in this life. It does not have to control me or shut me down. God's character is revealed in this, as He identifies with us in our hurtful experiences, as He transforms the rejection into something of eternal value, something that will be part of our credentials and eventually the jewels in our crown. It is a sign of our true relationship with Him, that He is more important than the things of this world.

Perhaps Paul knew what he was talking about when he said in Romans 8:16–17, *"The Spirit himself testifies with our spirit that we are God's children. And if we are God's children, then we are heirs of God and co-heirs with Christ, if indeed we share in His sufferings in order that we may share in His glory."* On several occasions, Paul refers to his rejections and sufferings as *"momentary afflictions,"* like they are no big deal compared to the incredible joy and glory of being God's kids.

While on a trip a few years back, God showed me that my heart was more healed than I realized. When I found myself in the middle of a hurtful experience between several good friends, I realized it didn't crush me or take me out. In the past, I would have felt crushed, and it might have taken years to recover from the hurt; but no longer. God helped me to reframe the experience, to not take offense, and to go to Him with my heart needs and allow Him to give me His perspective and to comfort my heart.

There is always more to the story than we can know. He helped me resist the old ungodly belief that people will always reject me (just like my friends here) and reframe it into the belief that even what the enemy means for evil, God will turn into something good. What a difference a matter of perspective makes.

I hope you will be encouraged as you read this, knowing that He wants to reframe the hurts of your life into something of value that you can embrace as a treasure. It makes it all worthwhile somehow in the end. I want to embrace it all and remember it as a gift (not a punishment), knowing it is all a matter of perspective, and I want to have His perspective.

Revelation #24: *Failure: A Necessary pre-requisite for humility.*

> *"For all of us have sinned and fallen short of the glory of God"* —Romans 3:23

Who of us, if honest, ever wants to fail, at anything? Yet, failure and mistakes and loss are a normal and healthy part of the growth process. How is it we are so averse to failing? It's created a generation that's not willing to try anything because they are too afraid of failing. When we aim high, we may not always meet the mark. But when we aim low or at nothing, we are always going to hit the mark. If Ben Franklin had quit after only 9,999 failures, we wouldn't have the lightbulb. If Gideon had quit after only one fleece, would he have become the *"mighty man of valor"* the angel addressed him as? (Judges 6:12) If Peter had told Jesus, "I'm too great a sinner to ever be used again because I betrayed you," could he have become Peter, the Rock, the key leader of the early church?

During a recent ministry session, the Lord showed a ministry receiver a great truth that addressed this issue. (They have given us permission to share this.) Like most of us, they had experienced many hurts and failures and losses in their life. In their time of receiving, God said to them that in order to grow spiritual muscles there needed to be resistance to create growth and strength. God basically said, "Failure equals resistance training!" It is an absolute necessity to have resistance as part of a healthy course of training, developing strength and capability to do a task or skill. It's no different in the spiritual realm of life.

When I talk about failure, I'm not talking primarily about intentional sin or moral failure but about simply making mistakes or being wrong about something or missing the mark somehow. Sometimes what we deem as failures may be a sin, but is it something that shuts us down or takes us out? Or that we should feel guilty or ashamed about? Is it unforgivable? The bigger question might be, "What did we learn from it?"

I remember as a teenager being taken skiing and falling down a lot! But the man who took me encouraged me with the words, "If you're not falling down, you're not growing or trying something harder." He gave me permission to not be perfect, to fail even, and there was no shame associated with it. It also reminds me of when Lee Iacoca, former CEO of Chrysler, replied when he was asked, "How did you become so successful?" His reply was, "I failed my way to the top."

When you look at most of the biblical characters, especially King David, we see people who blew it in just about every way possible; but God was able to take even their greatest failures and turn them into something valuable. God looked at their heart, not just their behavior. He always provides a way to learn and grow from our mistakes. God wants us to be able to see our part in any situation, including the failures. He wants us to learn to see the entire picture and to take responsibility for our part in it. What is so cool is that no matter how great we think our failures are, His grace is always greater.

When you look at your child or someone you love, do you just see their failures? Or do you see the whole person, all they can become, and the character of their hearts? If we as mere humans can do it, how come we think so little of God, believing He only see our faults and failures? His lens for us is always through Papa's love, His grace, and who He knows He created us to be. Perhaps, if we could learn to see ourselves through His lens, we could see even our failures as a gift that leads us to greater life, truth, and humility. It's a great equalizer. And it helps us know that there is not one of us "who is without sin" and has a right to "cast the first stone," like the Pharisees did with the woman caught in adultery (Jn 8:7).

Our righteousness is as filthy rags (Isa 64:6). Our success is not in our good works (that we might be tempted to take credit for through pride and performance), though we were created for good works (Eph 2:10). Our value or worth is not in our accomplishments. But He has given to us as a gift: His righteousness (2 Cor 5:21). It is truly a gift, and He invites us to receive it, that we might be changed by it, for we were created for righteousness and holiness. He says to seek it out above all else (Matt 6:33).

Failure is certainly not the end goal of our life; rather, the goal is to become all that He created us to become. When we see our lives as a failure, we often see God as a failure, that He messed up when He made us, that others are good while we are bad, and so forth. There is often a sense of shame and rejection we feel when we believe these lies about our identity. And we are often quick to point them out about others as well.

So, what's it going to be? Are we going to wallow in self-pity because of our failures or are we going to learn from them? Whether it is a big failure or a little failure, whether it is truly a sin or only a mistake, are we learning and growing and seeing even these areas of our lives as a rich treasure ground for nuggets of wisdom and truth? Enjoy the treasure hunt as you allow Him to use everything in your life for your good, even the failures. "*I will cause ALL things to work together for good; even what the enemy meant for evil, I will turn into something good* (of eternal value)" (Rom 8:28; Phil 1:6).

Revelation #25: *CHANGE: the great equalizing process of transformation.*

"Do not be conformed to the patterns of this world but be transformed by the renewing of your mind."
—Romans 12:2

Every single one of us needs to be supernaturally changed, in order to be conformed into the image of Christ. This is a great equalizer. There is not one of us who doesn't need to change. But who does the work? Can you change yourself? Are you smart enough or powerful enough to make it happen on your own? No, you're not. He is the only one big enough and able to do the work. He is the *"author and perfecter of our faith"* (Heb 12:2). He is the one who will *"finish the good work I have begun in you"* (Phil 1:6).

God invites us into the process and asks our permission to do the change. He alone can do the work of change in you, but He always asks our permission to allow Him to do the work. Because He is a gentleman and honors our free will, He wants our permission to freely do the work in us He knows we need. He has always been this way, starting with Adam and Even in the Garden.

Isn't it interesting how we often pray for Him to change us, to fix us, to make us different, to make our decisions for us? When we pray like this, we are asking Him to override our free will. I've heard many people voice that they don't even want free will because they don't think they can make a good decision for themselves. Wow! What we often forget is that He needs our permission to do the work of change. If He was to override our free will and make us do something against our will, He would then become our abuser or controller. And He will never do that because of His character.

There is no shortage of people who are happy to tell us what to do or to control us but not Him. And to add insult to injury, when He doesn't answer our prayer to force us to change, the accuser jumps on board and says, *"Boy, you must be really bad for God not to heal you, deliver you, or fix you."* And we often agree, building even more walls of mistrust and resentment with God, while making agreements with Satan and not even knowing it.

The passage of Romans 12:1–2 *("Do not be conformed to this world but be transformed by the renewing of your mind…")* was the first sermon I ever preached on when I was twenty-one years old. I didn't have a clue what I was talking about. I read a few commentaries and tried to make some sense of it all. But it's only been in the last few years I am beginning to see and understand more of what this really means and how it applies to my life.

I remember reading a book about wineskins by a popular author of the day, Keith Miller. In it, he refers to Matthew 9:17 and a well-known truth of that day that you don't put new wine into old wineskins, or it will be destroyed; that you will lose both the wine and the skin. When we as ministers try to force someone to change (either in belief or behavior), even if it seems to be for their good, it is like putting wine into an old wineskin. When we try to force someone to receive the Holy Spirit, it can be like trying to put new wine into old wineskins. God needs to do a work of change into the old wineskin to prepare it to receive the new wine (new revelation and truth).

Change is one of the things we resist the most. We prefer the familiar and what we know. We are even sometimes terrified of change. Why is that? Do you think we are getting some help from the accuser? The term "comfort-zone" isn't about comfort at all but familiarity. Why is it that someone who was abused as a child marries an abusive spouse? We often choose what is bad for us because it is familiar to us. But God says that unless we change and are *"reborn,"* we cannot enter the Kingdom of heaven. That sure freaked out the Pharisees of the day.

What does He need to change in you or me? Does He have our permission? He is waiting, inviting, and welcoming us into this new place. Are we willing? Can we trust He wants only the best for us? That He will use everything in our life for good, *"even what the enemy meant for evil"*? (Gen 50:20).

One of my favorite Skit Guys routines is called "The Chisel," and it's about letting God change us. In a very humorous way, they help us see how God is inviting each of us individually to let Him do the work of change. We often don't even know the areas that need the most work, much less how to go about doing it; but He does.

God is always gracious and gentle and patient in this process. How fast or slow it goes is often determined by our willingness or ability to fully trust Him and let Him be God, to let Him do what He does best. He is inviting each of us into this place of wholeness, of sanctification, of being *"prepared to be the bride."* I hope you will answer His invitation with a "Yes, and Amen!" but the Choice is always yours.

CHAPTER 7

RELATIONSHIP

Revelation #26: *Internal vs. External Processing – knowledge that can heal your relationship.*

"Let all that you do be done in love." —I Corinthians 16:14

W e have worked with hundreds of marriages, and one of the areas of conflict that has created inordinate amounts of pain and even led to separation is the area of how we process our thoughts and feelings. When someone processes either internally or externally, there is a belief grid that goes with it. It causes one to interpret what the other person is saying or meaning through that grid, and they are not usually the same.

One man put it this way, "My wife is an external processor. I am an internal processor." Translation: "She likes to talk through things; I like to go away and think for a while and then come back and talk once I've got it all figured out." The external wants to engage and the internal wants to escape in order to figure it out. If one or both come to the relationship with a belief that conflict is bad and must be avoided at all costs, then this makes it even harder to actually talk about the issue or check out what the other means, causing even more hurt and misunderstanding.

The reason I'm bringing this up is because it is an area of conflict based on misunderstanding and a different perspective of what someone else's words mean. The demonic, especially Leviathan (the king of pride and twisted communications) loves to use this to create confusion, conflict, and pain.

I speak from personal experience. In my first marriage, I was primarily an external processor, and my wife was almost exclusively an internal processor. This one area of our communications caused more strife, pain, and misunderstanding than just about anything. By the time I learned about this processing issue, there was so much pain and water under the bridge that we could never recover from it. But not so for others, I hope.

For an internal processor (generally), before they verbalize anything, they have diligently thought through all the possibilities of what would be best and what it would mean and how someone might interpret it, and so forth. By the time they are ready to share it, it is already a finished product that requires no discussion, questions, or nothing else. They expect the person to just accept it at face value for what it is, no questions asked.

For an external processor (usually), they prefer to process information outside with others. When they say something or verbally process, it is still just information to them, and they want to consider all the angles with someone else's help, before deciding what they want to receive for their own belief system. Just because they throw out an idea or verbalize something does not mean they believe it.

Each person tends to think that the other person will think and process the way they do, but this is not so. When an external processor hears the internal processor, they will ask questions and want to know how they came up with that thought or idea. They will proceed to challenge it, ask about it, question how they came up with it, and so forth. And to them that's perfectly normal and healthy. But to the internal processor, they perceive all these questions as an interrogation and a tearing down of their ideas or thoughts, which they have already meticulously thought through and which require no more discussion. They may react (internally or externally) with the thoughts, *"How dare they? Don't they care about me? What are they doing?"* and so forth. They might feel hurt and attacked and confused. This feeds their rejection or wounding issues and leads them to form judgments or ungodly beliefs about the external processor.

When the external processor shares their ideas and thoughts, the internal processor will be thinking that the external processor actually believes what they are saying and will often respond with shock or surprise or confusion. *"How can they possibly believe that?"* they might think to themselves but won't verbalize it. And when they respond with coolness, or don't join in the dialog or discussion, the external processor is thinking, *"Why won't they communicate with me? Why won't they help process with me what I'm trying to figure out? Don't they care?"* And they start making judgments of their own about the internal processor, and the war is on. All of this can be going on without either party knowing it.

Keep in mind that these are generalizations of one's preference for communication processing. It doesn't mean we are not capable of doing both or of learning both. And it is all in a spectrum, from one extreme to the other. Depending where we are on that spectrum can be an indicator of how much it is affecting our relationships, and if it is a potential problem that needs to be addressed as to how each person understands the other.

As we have worked with couples with conflict issues, just having this understanding about each other has helped many be able to reframe what they were believing about their spouse, to pay attention to the heart of their partner, and check out what they meant rather than being hurt by it or being too quick to judge. There is much more one needs in order to have good and open communications, but this is certainly one area that can be healed and resolved just by knowing it is there and not cooperating with it.

If this resonates in your spirit as an area of conflict in your own relationship, know that you can begin to learn each other's style and change how you see each other or listen to each other. This is where effective listening and feedback skills will benefit you greatly. Always check out what the other really means by something, and don't assume anything. You know what assuming does, right? It makes an A_ _ out of U and ME! ☺ I hope this is helpful and will benefit you in all your relationships.

Revelation #27: *Judgments: Our #1 Defense mechanism*

"Bitter roots are our sinful reactions and our con-demning judgments of people, and our refusal and inability to forgive. They are our reaction/response in our spirit to what is done to us. We then develop an expectancy that others will do the same to us, a self-fulfilling prophecy." —John Sandford

God has a lot to say in the Word about judgments:

"Judge not lest you be judged" (Matt 7:1); *"For at whatever point you judge another, you are condemning yourself, because you who pass judgment do the same things"* (Rom 2:1); *"Why do you look at the speck of sawdust in your brothers' eye and pay no attention to the plank in your own eye?"* (Matt 7:3); *"Do not judge*

and you will not be judged. Do not condemn and you will not be condemned" (Luke 6:37); *"Every tongue that rises up in judgment against you, you shall condemn!"* (Is 54:17); and the list goes on.

Basically, judgments are the walls of self-protection that we build (with the enemy's help), in order to protect ourselves from further hurt, rejection, or pain. When we make judgments, we initially feel safer, more powerful, even more just. But ultimately, we are just building walls that become thicker over time, that separate us from others, and even hinder our ability to hear God.

When people encounter our judgments, it's like bumping into a brick wall, and there is an *"ouch"* factor. These walls are invisible, but when someone tries to get close, they can feel them. It can create confusion and pain, which acts like a force that pushes others away. Usually, we don't even know these walls are there, or we believe we are doing such a good job of disguising it that no one could possibly know. But they do.

One of the early pioneers of Healing and Deliverance ministries, John Sandford (Elijah House ministries), has some core teaching about judgments and how they usually come out of bitter roots. They are a way we take back control after experiencing something hurtful and how we decide or vow to not let anyone do it to us again. There is often some unforgiveness, hurt, anger, or trauma that is unhealed or even buried very deep in our heart or memories. This bitter root allows demonic spirits to continue to torment us, to convince us of the need to build these walls as a way of surviving, whatever our perceived pain or offense. What I often share with couples having trust and intimacy issues, "survival skills do *not* work in intimacy." When we live in survivor mode, we can't get close to anyone, or them to us.

This becomes then, the crucial point of choice. Do I trust only in my survival instincts by building walls or do I learn to trust in God's protection and provision instead? This is often an indicator of the level of healing still needed in a persons' life. It is crucial for us to realize that these walls we have built don't actually work, and eventually they will steal our relationships and even our life. We need something more, something better, and we need to be willing to choose a different path for ourselves if we want to really live and enjoy life. This is His high invitation to choose a different path. What we often tell our receivers is that God is inviting us to live a Micah 6:8 life, *"He has shown you O mortal what is good. And what does the Lord require of you? To act justly, to love mercy, and to walk humbly with your God."*

How will you respond to His invitation? He asks us to be just, even when we are not treated justly, to love others even when we are not loved, to be kind and honest, even when others are not. Is this fair? Or is this God's way of calling us higher and to know what walking on the higher path really means? I welcome you to explore this with Him and decide for yourself what path you are willing to take with Him. Whatever you do, stay on His path, and it will be a good one.

Revelation #28: *Truth without Love / Love without Truth: a Hammer vs. a Wet Noodle*

"Rather, speaking the truth in love, we are to grow up in every way into Him who is the Head, into Christ, from whom the whole body, joined and held together by every joint with which it is equipped, when each part is working properly, makes the

body grow so that it builds itself up in love." —
Ephesians 4:15–16

*"Love without truth is sentimentality; it supports
and affirms us but keeps us in denial about our
flaws. Truth without love is harshness; it gives
us information but in such a way that we cannot
really hear it. Truth without love is imperious
self-righteousness. Love without truth is cowardly
self-indulgence."* —Timothy Keller

*"Truth without love is brutality, and love without
truth is hypocrisy."* –Warren Wiersbe

As we minister to people, we have found that we need to be both direct as well as kind, in order to build trust with them. They can't be healed of something they are not willing to see or acknowledge. In order to build trust, we need them to know we are not sitting in judgment of them and that they can feel safe to share even their worst failures and sins. We often say, "We are here to expose the enemy, not you!" We want them to be able to see how they have been set up, so they are willing to invest and cooperate in their own healing.

Most of us have probably heard the phrase "Would you rather be right or happy?" Our need to be right is often a stumbling block to creating true intimacy and can often be wounding and hurtful to the other person. If the core message of Ephesians 4 is about unity and healthy functioning relationship, then caring for each part while fulfilling our created purpose will be the highest goal. Does a healthy body reject or tear itself down? Or does it work hard for the good of the whole body, to *"build itself up in love"*?

We were watching a good movie recently, *Wonder*, and in it the teacher was teaching a precept that went like this, "If you have to choose between being right and being kind, be kind." Some believe that we are obligated to tell the truth, regardless of the cost, and that it has to do with one's integrity and character. "Honesty is the best policy," and such, we almost take pride in the fact that we are "truth-tellers" and "there is no deceit within us." We saw this "separatist" kind of thinking in the moral majority movement, where they felt it was their duty to point out everyone else's sin and condemn them for it. But in truth, when we know as little as we know, like it says in I Corinthians 13, then how can we be so adamant to hold on to such absolutes about our thinking, especially in how we judge one another?

At the other end of the spectrum, some think loving means not confronting or hurting someone else's feelings and that it is somehow unkind to share what is wrong with someone or how they are hurting themselves or others. They turn a blind eye to the offense and act as if it never happened. Somehow, that equates to "turning the other cheek," to "being the better man," and so forth.

Perhaps the greater question might be, "What is the message in my heart I want the other person to receive? And how will they be able to receive it? What is the content of my message? And how is it to be delivered? What is the character of my heart as the deliverer of the message?"

How did God deliver His message of love and salvation to us? Certainly not in the way we would probably have expected. He sent His only Son to suffer and die on our behalf to pay the blood price for our debt. It should make us do a double take about what kind of message we're sending and how is it being received.

Truth and love are a necessary combination to not only bring an honest message but to bring it in such a way it doesn't create a defensive reaction that stops the receiver from receiving its true heart meaning. It is our personal goal to communicate in such a way, with the leading and power of the Holy Spirit, humbling ourselves to the truth that we are all equal before Him and in need of the same healing. I have been blessed to experience this from some of my leaders. Even when they brought correction, it felt good because I felt loved. That is a test we can use when we listen to critical voices, is there a spirit of love and gentleness in the correction? If so, then you can probably trust that is from the Holy Spirit and not from the accuser.

I like to use the analogy that truth without love is like a big hammer and does more harm than good; while love without truth is like a wet noodle, lacking any body or substance or impact for real change. No matter how we want to spin it, we need both attributes in our language and in our hearts if we want to communicate the complete truth of God's love and His desire for our freedom and wholeness. I encourage you all to keep growing in this area and to not give up on communicating the truth in your heart, as you let His divine love fill you and guide you into all wisdom and truth.

CHAPTER 8

DISCIPLESHIP

Revelation #29: *Welcoming His presence is a __choice__ to respond to His invitation.*

"Behold, I stand at the door and knock. If anyone hears my voice and opens the door, I will come in and sup with him..." —Revelation 3

W hat does it mean to have Jesus in our hearts? Is it just a cute turn of phrase? Or is it a relational reality? It always amazes me how many people were taught this scripture as part of evangelism, when in fact it was written to believers, describing a personal invitation to have ongoing relationship with a living God named Jesus, doing the one common thing we do more than breathing, that of sharing a meal.

Isn't it interesting that one of the key tenants of Christian practice and faith is the Lord's Supper, a common yet intimate event. When is the last time you shared a meal with Jesus? When the two guys on the road to Emmaus were walking with a stranger, they didn't know it was Jesus until they had a meal together. (Luke 24:13-35) Then, their eyes were enlightened, and they rejoiced in His presence. Every time we eat, we are reminded of the sacrifice He made for us out of His great love; that the purpose of His sacrifice was that we might be restored to intimate and eternal life in His presence.

I don't know about you, but I eat plenty. What a better way to help me remember Him than to associate Him with food. How much time do we think about food? A lot! And how many of us have food issues? There is something so intimate and cozy and satisfying about eating and sharing a meal. Do you think that's why He associates the Cross and the Blood with such an intimate and personal event as the Last Supper? Maybe He knew what He was doing when He chose that imagery and activation for us to remember what He has done for us.

It's His daily, hourly invitation to hang out with Him, to enjoy Him, to be nourished by Him, and to share our lives with Him (from the simple to the sublime—He loves it all). I welcome you to His table, to open the door and let Him in, to make Him not only a guest at your table, but an honored guest. I pray that food and meals may take on a whole new meaning when we partake together with Him and the life that He offers. *"He who eats of me will never hunger or thirst again"* (Jn 6).

Revelation #30: *Qualities that reveal the nature of a true disciple of Christ.*

"If you hold to my teaching, you are truly my disciples. THEN you will know the truth, and the truth will set you free." —John 8:31–32 (NIV)

Most of us only hear one part of that scripture, *"The truth will set you free."* And we assume that if we just agree with whatever we think is the "truth," then we are free and clear. The question we *don't* ask is, "What does it take to know the truth?" We often forget that the road to understanding the truth starts with obedience. In truth, we don't have a clue what the truth is until we start on the road of obedience. As we take that step of faith, He begins to reveal to us His truth. And as we continue down the road of truth, we encounter freedom in the person and presence of Jesus through His Spirit. *"I am the Way, the TRUTH, and the life; no one comes to the Father except through me"* (Jn 14:6).

What does it really mean to be a disciple of Christ? Are there any credentials required to become one of His disciples? How does one tell whether you are truly one of His disciples or not?

It seems to me that in order to be His disciple, it starts with faith, trust, and simple obedience. It's not just having the right theology or the right answers. It's not just saying a prayer and then doing what we want to do anyway. It requires listening, observing, learning, growing, stepping out, activating our faith, and following Him. That sounds a lot like what Jesus' disciples did centuries ago. Has it really changed that much? How do we learn? How do we follow someone who is dead and gone?

In John's gospel, chapters 14–17, Jesus talks to His disciples about what is about to happen to Him and to prepare them for their life ahead without His physical presence. They had enjoyed His daily presence for three years, and now they were about to experience the greatest pain and loss of their lives. He says, *"I tell you the truth, I must go that the Spirit of truth might come to you…; and when he comes, he will guide you into all truth"* (Jn 16:6–15).

In John 15:8–17, He says, *"Bear much fruit, showing your-selves to be my disciples…remain in my love… that your joy may be complete…you are my friends if you do what I command… everything I have learned from the Father I have made known to you…I chose you and appointed you to go and bear fruit…this is my command: love one another."*

We are in a generation of New Agers that say, "Truth is whatever you want it to be. There is no absolute truth." Just like the Church, truth is a person, not a theology or an ideology or a collection of information. Truth is in the person of Jesus Christ, and He sent the Spirit of God to *"lead us into all truth."* Truth is in a relationship and intimacy with a living being, not in head knowledge or book knowledge. There is no room for pride or self-will or performance or smarts. It is about humility, obedience, trust, wisdom, and grace.

If you are truly a disciple, will you not reflect the one you are following? Have you learned and grown and been transformed into the likeness of the one you follow? It is on the journey that truth becomes known. We don't start with truth; we begin with obedience to His commands. And as we stay on His path, we bump into truth without even realizing it. Being a disciple means we trust completely in the one we follow. What is He asking you to do? And have you followed His instructions? Or do you argue and debate and wrestle with Him? I encourage you to take the leap and to step onto His path. It's quite an adventure being a disciple of Jesus Christ of Nazareth. And it's worth the cost of a ticket, your very life.

Revelation #31: The prayers of the 'Righteous' make ALL the Difference!

"Confess your sins one to another and pray for one another that you may be healed. For the fervent prayers of a righteous man availeth much…"
—James 5:16

Recently, during some trying times, my pastor reminded me of this verse. As I thought about it, I realized the power was not in me or my righteousness but that of Christ, who has imputed to me His righteousness. He says that my righteousness is as *"dirty rags"* (Is 64:6). But the righteousness of God is my inheritance and my identity in Christ. (Is 54:17 & 2 Cor 5:21). If that's the case, then every believer's prayers are powerful, and we should expect amazing results. Revelation says that *"The prayers of the saints are the incense before His throne"* (Rev 8:4). We know that He hears them all, that He catches them, and that He responds quickly. *"Before a word is even on my tongue, He knows it already"* (Ps 139:4)

Wow, is that really true? God's answered prayers have a lot more to do with His righteousness and who He is than with me being so powerful. But what is my part? The other word from James 5:16 that stands out, is "fervent" (diligent, or steadfast, or enduring.) When I hear that, I'm reminded of I Thessalonians 5:17, to *"pray without ceasing."* That sounds a lot like fervent, doesn't it? There is a fortitude, a strength of will, a faithfulness, a stick-to-it-iveness; to never give up, to trust in the promise and the promise giver, to press through until the battle is won, to finish the race and not quit. You name it, there are a lot of ways it talks about staying on His journey and not giving up or giving in. This is the fervor of prayer that He is talking about, and it has powerful results.

There is great freedom in knowing that God is the one responsible for the release of healing and deliverance and that it is not based on my perfection or performance or even my own personal goodness. That was a releasing word for me to want to pray even more for people and to see their release and healing and to increase my faith in God's promises to *"finish the good work He has begun in each of us"* (Phil 1:6). But it is also important to note that the power of our prayers has as much to do with staying in His presence and activating our love with our words as it is resting in His promises and agreeing with His truths in an intentional and specific way.

God is certainly not a vending machine, and our prayers are not some bargaining chip to try and buy what we want. Our loving Father loves for us to call on Him and to seek Him for the treasure and the gift that He so eagerly is waiting to bestow upon us, our healing and our restoration as His sons and daughters. He loves it when we ask and expect big things of Him, because it sends the message that we know that He is a big God and we honor Him as we do this. It also stretches our faith muscles and is part of our obedience as His disciples, to love others and to pray for them with sacrifice and fervency and dedication.

From start to finish, God is in it all. The praying person, the beneficiary of the prayers, and the onlookers are all part of the drama that is unfolding. And it becomes the testimonies of God's goodness in the earth. Praise God! Praise Him in His sanctuary! Praise Him in everything! When He says to give thanks for everything, He's not kidding. Everything is working together for our good, even the hard stuff.

So, don't give up! It's not religion, it's relationship. It's not duty, it's devotion. It's not a burden, it's a blessing. Our prayers are powerful. They are simply God's ways of using our words and our will to release His ultimate purpose and plans to heal His kids in every way possible. We all get blessed. We can't out-give God. The more we sow seeds of sweet faith, love, and devotion, the more we reap His avalanche of joy and blessing.

Don't get me wrong, this is not as easy as it seems. I remember one time when I was complaining about someone and judging their immaturity and lack of growth, and God asked me if I would be willing to sacrifice one day of devoted prayer for them. At first, I was irritated, but my little imp of self-righteousness said, "How hard can that be?" It was one of the hardest days I have ever experienced. I went to the Grotto in Portland, a beautiful and peaceful place where I could devote myself to prayer and intercession. I was good for about an hour before I started getting antsy, bored, and impatient. After three hours, it was almost unbearable, and I thought I would never be able to make a full day. I lasted six hours before I finally went home. I was humbled beyond words. God taught me a hard lesson that day, that I should not be so quick to judge or to think I know what's in Another person's heart. But instead, to turn to Him and ask HOW I might pray and for His will to be done in their lives, not mine. When He says to *"pray without ceasing..."* (I Thess. 5:16), it's hard to believe that it is even humanly possible. As I grow in my trust of His character and His Word, I am learning that this phrase is mostly about hanging out with Him and coming into agreement with His heart; THEN, to activate it with my voice!

It has been a journey of changing what I believe about prayer, coming to understand it's about being with Him, speaking directly and honestly, listening with a heart of peace, and having a joyous expectancy to receive Him as my friend, companion, and lover. It is worth it all. Bless you as you release your prayers with power and honesty and expectancy, trusting the God who loves to bless you beyond measure!

ABOUT THE AUTHOR

Brian Jacobson and his wife Linda – Co-founders of His Heartministers LLC, and full-time ordained ministers with Restoring the Foundations International. Originally from Oregon and Washington, they moved to North Carolina to join the RTF family to help bring healing to the Bride of Christ. They have thirty-plus years of counseling and healing ministry experience and been married over twenty years. Brian got his BA in vocal performance and MA in church music from Seattle Pacific University and then an M-Div. from Fuller Seminary. Brian directed a half-way house with Good Samaritan Ministries, pastored for five years, and supervised counseling and prayer ministry with House of Myrrh for many years. For the past fourteen years, they have been teaching, training, and ministering with Restoring the Foundations, sharing and imparting God's revelation of healing and deliverance. They have been privileged to minister to individuals and families from over forty-five countries, as well as gaining a reputation for seeing broken marriages restored.

My own journey of divorce, betrayal, an alcoholic father, addiction and Brokenness have served as part of my testimony of healing as well as giving me the compassion and credentials to understand others in their brokenness, without judgment. Having almost died of pancreatitis, along with seeing my wife almost die of a stroke, has forced me to look at my deepest fears and to find freedom from them. God gifted me with teaching and writing skills, which others have encouraged me to share. I resisted this task until my wife suggested I start by writing one revelation or story at a time. This book is a result of that encouragement. Linda and I continue to minister, teach, and train, sharing with others the Heart of God to hundreds of broken people, one at a time.

With gratitude to my savior and healer, Jesus Christ,
Brian

If you wish to find out more about Brian and Linda's ministry, check out their website: HisHeartministers.com or email them at Heartministers@yahoo.com. You can also see their Minister profile on Restoringthefoundations.org.

CPSIA information can be obtained
at www.ICGtesting.com
Printed in the USA
LVHW071611220520
656048LV00003BA/271